Job

Self Development Guide to Answering Even the Toughest Questions

(Guide to a Winning Interview With Amazing Interview Answers With Perfect Body Language)

Marc Franson

Published by Rob Miles

Marc Franson

All Rights Reserved

Job: Self Development Guide to Answering Even the Toughest Questions (Guide to a Winning Interview With Amazing Interview Answers With Perfect Body Language)

ISBN 978-1-989990-76-6

All rights reserved. No part of this guide may be reproduced in any form without permission in writing from the publisher except in the case of brief quotations embodied in critical articles or reviews.

Legal & Disclaimer

The information contained in this book is not designed to replace or take the place of any form of medicine or professional medical advice. The information in this book has been provided for educational and entertainment purposes only.

The information contained in this book has been compiled from sources deemed reliable, and it is accurate to the best of the Author's knowledge; however, the Author cannot guarantee its accuracy and validity and cannot be held liable for any errors or omissions. Changes are periodically made to this book. You must consult your doctor or get professional medical advice before using any of the suggested remedies, techniques, or information in this book.

Upon using the information contained in this book, you agree to hold harmless the Author from and against any damages, costs, and expenses, including any legal fees potentially resulting from the application of any of the information provided by this guide. This disclaimer applies to any damages or injury caused by the use and application, whether directly or indirectly, of any advice or information presented, whether for breach of contract, tort, negligence, personal injury, criminal intent, or under any other cause of action.

You agree to accept all risks of using the information presented inside this book. You need to consult a professional medical practitioner in order to ensure you are both able and healthy enough to participate in this program.

Table of Contents

INTRODUCTION 1

CHAPTER 1: BASED ON THE COUNT OF PEOPLE INVOLVED 3

CHAPTER 2: EMPOWERING YOUR SKILLS AND KNOW-HOW 10

CHAPTER 3: THE INTERVIEW PREPARATION PROCESS 15

CHAPTER 4: WHAT TO DO 33

CHAPTER 5: THE ESSENTIALS OF A STAR BEHAVIORAL INTERVIEW 38

CHAPTER 6: NAILING THE INTERVIEW 56

CHAPTER 7: 10 TOUGHEST JOB INTERVIEW QUESTIONS.. 67

CHAPTER 8: FIRST IMPRESSIONS 74

CHAPTER 9: DRESSING FOR THE INTERVIEW 82

CHAPTER 10: MAINTAINING MOTIVATION 89

CHAPTER 11: COMPANY AND INDUSTRY QUESTIONS 95

CHAPTER 12: QUESTIONS YOU SHOULD ASK 99

CHAPTER 13: HOW TO MAKE THE MOST OF YOUR RESUME, EVEN IF YOU ARE UNDERQUALIFIED 103

CHAPTER 14: ETIQUETTE AT JOB INTERVIEW 110

CHAPTER 15: REMEMBERING THE BASICS 118

CHAPTER 16: HOW MUCH SHOULD YOU TELL DURING THE INTERVIEW? 124

CHAPTER 17: DEVELOPING THE LETTER OF INTRODUCTION 131

CHAPTER 18: THE #1 MISTAKES TO AVOID DURING AN INTERVIEW 147

CHAPTER 19: HOW NOT TO OBSESS AFTER THE INTERVIEW 150

CHAPTER 20: AFTER THE INTERVIEW 154

CHAPTER 21: PREPARING FOR YOUR JOB INTERVIEW ... 158

CHAPTER 22: INTERVIEW SKILLS INTRODUCTION 165

CHAPTER 23: POSSIBLE ANSWERS JUST TO GUIDE FOR INTERVIEWEES. 170

CHAPTER 24: INTERVIEWING THE INTERVIEWER 178

CHAPTER 25: LEAVE YOUR QUESTIONS FOR LAST 185

CHAPTER 26: THE "UNEMPLOYMENT" JOB DESCRIPTION 196

CONCLUSION 202

Introduction

When you hear the word Human Resources, what comes to mind? Before starting in this profession, I had no idea what human resources was, did, or even why they were called human resources to begin with. To be honest, I still haven't quite figured out the latter, but after graduating college and having built my career in HR, I have a clearer and more hands-on understanding of what we are and what exactly it is we do. Human Resources is one of the more abstract and complex part of any organization. We are constantly changing and updating with laws as they are passed. Whether or not there's a sign on the door, every company has an HR department. Depending on the company size, human resources may be split up into various buckets. Sometimes, those buckets all pour into the same bucket and are filtered through one or two people, but ideally, HR should be handled by multiple professionals, each specializing in their particular area. These areas usually are comprised the following: talent acquisition or recruitment, compensation and benefits, payroll, and employee relations. Since this book is about getting the job you want, or at least an interview, we're going to focus on the recruitment side of human resources and discover the best ways to get a call, or a call back, from this department.

Chapter 1: Based On The Count Of People Involved

One-to-one interview (Personal interview): It is the most well-known among the interview types; it includes the interviewer posing inquiries perhaps both specialized and general, to the interviewee to examine how to fit the competitor is for the job.

Example: Posts in small organizations and mid-level and high-level jobs in big organizations.

Group interview:

This involves multiple candidates, and they are given a topic for discussion. They are assessed on their conversational ability and how satisfactorily they are able to have their own views and make others believe in them. Here, the best among the lot gets selected.

Example: Fresher posts and mid-level sales posts.

Panel interview (Committee Interview):

The interviewers here are group fr.om among the company people who are in a senior position, and usually, the panel interview is when the candidate is supposed to make a presentation. But many-a-times it could be for the job interview as well.

Example: Mid-level and high-level jobs.

BASED ON THE PLANNING INVOLVED

A structured interview (Formal interview or guided interview):

Here in the traditional form of an interview, the questions asked are all in a standard format, and the same is used for all the candidates. This is to assess the ability of all the candidates impartially.

Example: Entry-level jobs for fresher.

Unstructured interview (Informal interview or conversational interview):

This is the opposite of a structured interview. Here the interviewer has a definite idea in mind about the questions to be asked, but it doesn't follow a certain format. The interviewer may deviate, and a conversation type interview follows.

Example: Mid-level job interview for a managerial position

BASED ON JUDGING THE ABILITIES;

Behavioral-based interview:

The interviewee is asked questions about past work experiences and how it was dealt with in a particular situation. This helps the interviewer understand the candidate's future performance based on his past experiences. Here the candidates need to provide examples when they have handled situations. The probing may be in detail to assess the candidate's behavior and responses, and this determines the candidate's future job prospects.

Example: Interview for managerial positions, executive posts.

Problem-solving interview (Task-Oriented interview):

Here the interviewer is more concerned about the problem-solving abilities, be it technical, managerial, creative or analytical skills. This is the most common among the interview patterns, and it may involve either writing and answering a questionnaire set or answering the technical questions orally.

Example: Interviews for Software recruitments, technical industries, and managerial positions.

Depth interview (In-depth interview):

When you need to ascertain everything about the interviewee right from life history, academic qualifications, work experiences, hobbies, and interests, you conduct the depth interview.

Here the interviewer has a clear idea about the questions he will be asking, but once the question is asked, he allows the conversation to flow and is more of a listener. This interview takes time and more of a friendly approach of the interviewer towards the interviewee.

Example: For executive posts.

Stress interview:

Very rare, but such interviews are conducted to see how the candidate will be able to react in stressful situations and to assess if he will be able to handle the crisis at his job.

The tactics involved include:

Completely ignore the candidate by maybe, making a phone call in the middle of the interview.

Or some other tactic like continuously interrupting the candidate when he answers the questions.

Trying to enforce your point of view forcefully even if he disagrees.

Asking a whole lot of questions all at once.

Interrupting him by asking another question not related to his answer.

Example: For banker jobs.

BASED ON THE TASK

Apprenticeship interview:

Here the candidate is a novice, and the interview is a very formal one with general questions and some skill related questions being asked.

Example: Interview for training programs in organizations.

Evaluation interview:

In this interview, a fixed set of questions are asked, and a scoring system evaluates the points scored. This type of interview negates the scope of the personal bias of the interviewer.

Example: Interview in corporate organizations

Promotion interview:

This is for an employee of the company seeking a higher position for career enhancement purposes.

Example: Interviews in mid-level posts.

Counseling interview:

When employees are called, and their problems and solutions are discussed within the organization, such meeting type interviews are called counseling interviews.

Example: Interviews in big organizations

Disciplinary interview:

Here an individual or number of employees or sometimes the employee union is interviewed for their misconduct or non-performance. This is more sort of a meeting between the manager and the employees to get the problem resolved.

Example: Interviews in big companies.

Persuasive interview:

The interviewee here has to persuade the interviewer to accept his point of view as in case of an employee persuading his manager to implement some changes in the policy or a sales manager persisting on selling a product.

Example: Interviews in mid-level managerial posts

Chapter 2: Empowering Your Skills And Know-How

How many times have you applied for a job and failed to secure an interview, let alone get hired? Job seekers are always in a rush to craft and send in applications. Some people even craft and submit applications in a day even though the job interview is set to be conducted in two weeks time. It might be said that the early bird will always catch the worm, but sometimes, hurrying to do something like applying for a job can ruin your chances of ever being hired. Many mistakes in the application process will have ruined your chances of having a fair stab at the job. Ask yourself this question: are you truly qualified for the job, especially with regards to being endowed with the right skills? How much do you know about the job?

As discussed in the previous chapter, a company may decide to hire a novice who only has few years of working experience instead of going for that person with at least ten years of working experience. The question is, why?

Well, you can hardly crush a job interview if, despite the many years of experience you have had doing the same job in another organization, you never bothered with empowering your skills and know-how in the field. This brings us to this question: how should you empower your knowledge and skills? While skills and knowledge alone can help you stand out from the pack of equally competitive job applicants shortlisted for an interview, what have you done as far as broadening your knowledge and sharpening your skills are concerned? Discussed below are a few ways to empower your skills and knowledge so that the next time you apply for a job, you will not just secure an interview but go on to crush it.

Problem-solving skills

Employers will always be looking for people with great attention to detail and those who have the will and desire to perform a job well. There are always some interview questions requiring at least some problem solving. This should start you thinking. How many times have you helped solve a problem – not necessarily at the workplace, but also in real life situations? Did you succeed? There is no particular job that will never require problem-solving skills, which means that you should work on your aptitude skills no mater what sort of job you intend to apply for. During an interview, questions that seek to unearth your problem solving skills will definitely edge you out of an employment opportunity if you are ill prepared. This also means that you should be thinking on your feet and making sure that you always have effective suggestions ready at your fingertips for basic problematic scenarios. Problem-solving situations also require a critical thinker who can provide real solutions. Therefore, before your next job interview, cultivate the right skills on this.

Interpersonal skills

A workplace is made up of people from different walks of life and with different attitudes. How you relate to people really matters, especially when it comes to jobs such as sales and public relations that involve interacting with other people regularly. The only way you can develop your interpersonal skills is by always being positive, even to negative people. Further, everything you do from the moment you walk into the interviewing room and exchange pleasantries with the panel to the moment you leave and beyond will influence the panel's opinion of your interpersonal skills. Remember that there will be someone awarding points for every little thing you do right, from proper greetings to a proper posture while sitting down. Make this work for you.

Make good use of vocational training sessions and conferences

Seminars, conferences, and other types of vocational training sessions have been instrumental in the lives of many employees and would-be-employees. There is always something new that you can learn from training, as long as it is relevant to your area of specialization.

Also, any training that is tailored towards empowering your skills is something that you should go for.

Vocational trainings will always be an opportunity to broaden your knowledge on emerging issues and trends regarding job performance. This means that you should start looking out for seminars and conferences that would see you not only advance in your career, but also crush your next job interview. You could be the only person with such training or experience among several people shortlisted for the same job interview.

Chapter 3: The Interview Preparation Process

Preparing for success at your job interview involves many different factors. In addition to your impressive resume, which you've now optimized and have ready to go, you must also consider what type of clothing you're going to wear, the good and bad things you can say about yourself, and most importantly, how to channel your good and positive energy to give your interviewer a first impression of you that he won't soon forget.

Job search techniques undergo significant changes over time, and so does the labor market and all associated job descriptions. However, if there is one thing that remains a constant in the middle of all of this, it is the job interview process. This is the one opportunity you are given by your prospective employer to sell yourself.

While in an interview, it is the first 30 seconds that often prove to be the most important and can decide whether the rest of the process goes in your favor or against you. If you wish to see put yourself a cut above the rest, this is when you really need to get your game right. According to numerous business psychologists, the three Ps are crucial to your success in a job interview. You should be <u>prepared</u>, you should put in enough <u>practice</u>, and on the big day you really need to stand up and <u>perform</u>.

What to Wear

So, you finally have that much awaited job interview coming up tomorrow. You have done every bit of research on the organization, you are well prepared to face the questions that they put across to you, and you have also managed to reach the venue a few minutes ahead of schedule. Could you have been more ready?

Before you reach the interview location, you step into the restroom where you take one final look at yourself in the mirror. All of a sudden your mind races as you think to yourself, "Am I wearing the right kind of dress for this interview?"

While we always preach that we should never judge a book by its cover, human nature still dictates that appearance still makes a big difference in how your potential employer (or anyone else, for that matter) perceives you.

When you are going for an interview, you are basically marketing yourself as a product so it is important to keep the best possible image for yourself. You don't need to go out and buy the most expensive suits or get a big makeover to make an impression, though. As long as you do your homework and dress appropriately, you should be able to show your interviewer that you are professional and that you mean business.

Tip Number One: Asking What You Should Wear is Perfectly Alright

If you are appearing for an interview at one of the many traditional industries such as accounting and financing, an appropriate dress would be business professional attire – a conservative suit along with tie and shirt for a man while for a woman it can a conservative suit with jewelry and shirt that matches well with your personality.

For other industries such as information technology, graphic design, public relations, and advertising, there is no clear instruction on what employees need to wear. This is where the general dress policy of an organization comes into the picture and is something you can ask when you first get a call for an interview.

Asking the person who contacts you to schedule the interview more about the company culture so that you can dress properly for the interview is by no means a crime. On the contrary, it goes a long way towards showing respect for the organization in question.

If you still feel yourself harboring some doubt, then you can always choose to be cautious with your choice of words. You can say how in the past you have ended up being overdressed. This is a much better thing to do than showing up grossly underdressed and underprepared for the occasion.

Tip Number Two: Be Smart with Your Shopping

There is no need to buy a number of different suits while appearing for different interviews with the same organization. You can simply have one suit combined with something known as the "capsule dressing" strategy — this is a practice where you vary the accompanying dress with the suit on every instance.

For example, a young woman who has invested in a nice black pantsuit could make the most of that for her interviews while altering the accompanying scarf, jewelry, and shirt on each occasion.

Tip Number Three: There is no Need for Spending a Fortune

In order to get an idea of what is the ideal dress to wear in an interview, visit some high-end stores like Neiman Marcus or Nordstrom. However, if you feel you are somewhat short on cash, try purchasing your clothes from an outlet store.

When taking into account the clothes that you are likely to wear for an interview, pay greater focus on what the cost will be for every instance of wearing that piece of dress rather than on what the overall price tag looks like. You could be looking at a $150 trendy suit that you cannot wear on more than two instances every month for a couple of years. Here you will be dealing with a product that has a fairly high cost-per-wear.

However if you pick a $300 suit with a cut that is not so trendy, then you are likely to be able to wear it over a longer duration. Don't balk by simply taking a look at the original price tag; rather, give some thought on how long, and how often, you can get some good use out of the dress that you are buying.

Tip Number Four: Don't Overlook the Importance of Accessories

If you are wearing leather shoes to an interview make sure they have the proper kind of shine. In case you are wearing suede shoes, ensure that you have given them a good brushing. In the event that you have shoes that are older than five years, take them down to a shoemaker and get them worked on.

You can opt to carry a leather briefcase with you provided it is still in considerably good shape, but in the modern scenario this is not quite advisable. A better option would be to go with a nice portfolio binder.

You may be tempted to ask if all of this investment that you are making towards getting your professional image correct before an interview will pay any dividends at the actual event. Not only will this turn out to be helpful, but it is very much regarded as an essential part of all preparations that need to be taken for an interview.

Your image is a critical component in an interview because it shows the level of attention you pay to details. In addition, recruiters are able to get a better idea of the kind of representation you will give to the clients on behalf of their organization. This visual message has a significant influence on how your employer perceives you and can ultimately determine whether or not they think you are worthy of earning the job.

What NOT to Say

While you are out hunting for a suitable job, you may be led to think that getting a call for an interview is something of a major achievement. Usually it is true but in some of the cases this is a small step forward in the overall hiring process.

There are some jobs when you may be pitted against dozens of other interviewees so it is very important for you to be careful about what you say so that you are not at a risk of putting yourself at a disadvantage. There are some things that are proven interview-killers and you should take great care to ensure that you don't end up saying any of these while giving your interview.

"What sort of perks do you offer?"

Put off all talks about perks and benefits until you have reached the stage of negotiation. This is the part where you are given a clear indication that a job offer is in place. It could also come up prior to that if the interviewer decides to make a reference to that subject.

In a general discussion, an interviewer for a popular electronic products manufacturing firm said that one common question coming from most of the prospective employees is regarding the number of free products that they will be offered every year. If you happen to ask such questions during an interview, you can rest assured that your name will be put on the fast track to the rejection bin.

"What is the thing that your company really deals in?"

This is one question that managers and recruiters are bombarded with on almost every single occasion though you may find it very hard to believe. Before going ahead with a job interview, take some time out and research about the business interests and activities of the organization in question. Moreover, find some constructive ways in which you can help the company improve upon the things that it regularly deals in.

"My last boss was a real pain."

If you go around complaining about your former boss it only puts you in a very bad light. It could very well be the truth that you are telling but a prospective employer will think of it as a complaining attitude on your part.

A poor sport is not really the kind of person anyone takes an interest in working with. A better option would be to talk of the difficulties and challenges you came across in your previous appointment and how you overcame these to achieve positive results.

"I love your glasses!"

Complimenting any person in the interview panel on their physical appearance is a strict no-no. Many people can regard it as an inappropriate approach while for others it can be downright creepy. It is okay to pay someone a compliment but it should be something with respect to their professional capabilities. You can praise a recent success that the organization or the interviewer (if you know he is the person) has had, but no more than that.

"My feet are killing me!"

Saying that you are faced with some kind of physical discomfort will be looked upon as a sign of negativity. It may be interpreted as a habit that you will also bring in to your work life and complain about every time you are unable to put in a satisfactory performance.

It is not a good idea to say that you are feeling unwell for the interview because you were partying hard the previous night. No hiring manager is ever going to select you in such a scenario.

"I was fired from my last position…"

Lying while appearing for a job interview is never a good thing to do! Nevertheless, there are ways in which you can be more graceful while explaining that unhappy incident when you got fired from your previous employment.

You could highlight the fact that there were ideological differences between you and your boss regarding the focus of your respective department and then you decided that it was time to move on to a different role. Then, focus on your skills and work experience, and talk about why they are more suited to this new role that you are interviewing for.

"All I want is a job and it does not matter what job I am offered."

While this may not be any bit further from the truth, do you think it will really get you anywhere if you show yourself to be overly desperate? Not only does the interviewer want to know why you are appearing for the interview of that particular job role, he is also keen to see if you are the person who fits that position.

"I don't know..."

These three words should never be repeated over the course of a job interview even when you are dead sure that you are clueless about the answer to any particular question. It's better to say something like "I''ll try and find out the answer and get back to you towards the end of the day."

Sometimes, you will be asked hypothetical questions that may not directly deal with the job position, such as the number of golf balls to be required for filling up a certain vacant space. These questions are more aimed at finding out your thought processes, how you analyze problems, and how you come up with solutions. These don't come with a correct answer, but make sure you think about your answer carefully and come up with a solution that highlights your skills and experience.

"My biggest weakness is that I work too hard!"

Your interviewer has been taking interviews for way too long to know that this answer is a routine response. So when someone puts forward the question "What is your biggest weakness?", how do you go ahead and answer it?

Choose a response that does not have a direct relation to the job role for which you are appearing in the interview and show how you have taken measures to ensure there is an improvement in your weak area.

For example, you could say that you had a problem with speaking in front of large number of people. However, you addressed this issue by enrolling into Toastmasters and taking part in some voluntary projects where you had to talk in front of a number of people, such as a seminar. As a result, you can show the interview that not only do you proactively look to improve yourself, but that the weakness itself is improving by the day.

Building Up Your Positive Energy

Demonstrating yourself to be a very likeable person is important when you are appearing for an interview. Try to establish a connection with the interviewers rather than simply focusing on impressing them. In order to give yourself maximum amount of confidence, focus every bit of your energy on building a strong rapport with the interviewer rather than simply trying to impress the person.

There seems to be a misinterpretation among the masses that you show your confidence when you are able to dominate a conversation. In reality, it has more to do with your ability to put people at ease around yourself. This way you are better able to connect and work with others rather than simply putting the focus on yourself.

Breathing techniques help boost your confidence

Feeling relaxed is something that governs how confident you are at any given point in time. This is where mindfulness and breathing exercises can turn out to be extremely helpful. If you focus on nothing else but your breathing before you go in for an interview, it will go a long way towards soothing your nerves.

While in an anxious state, blood drains away from the brain which hampers our cognitive abilities. With the help of slow, deep breathing, the oxygen will flow back to your brain and allow you to think more clearly.

Be kind to yourself before appearing for an interview

Be compassionate towards yourself just as a friend would do before you go ahead and appear for an interview. This will help in dispelling the critical thoughts that could otherwise be a hindrance on your quest for success and glory.

Never hold back while selling yourself because the interviewer will only see what you show him. Often, candidates worry that they will end up sounding arrogant but you should remember that the members in the interview panel are no mind-readers. They don't have any other way of telling what you will be offering them so that onus is entirely on you.

Relaxation exercises and power poses can help curb anxiety

Put your focus entirely on the present moment. This is something that you can achieve by concentrating for a few moments on your breathing. It will be of immense help in calming you down.

In addition, try and focus on speaking slowly while giving the interview. It is human tendency to start speaking very fast while in a nervous state. Do not feel scared about putting some silence from time to time as this will only help improve your command over the entire situation.

Imagine a scenario where you emerge successful

Believing yourself to be the best person for the job and then settling into that confidence in a relaxed manner will only serve to elevate your level of confidence. When you picture yourself at an interview that ends in success, your self-esteem will register a significant boost.

Before imagining the successful interview process, visualize yourself in a situation in which you walked into the room, shook the hands of those in the interview panel, and then gave a confident answer to every question. This is the best technique you can use for calming every ounce of your pre-interview nerves.

Prepare your answers and rehearse them out loud

If you have answers prepared for most of the questions that you think are likely to appear in an interview, then it can help take the pressure off your shoulders. Being prepared is key because its benefits are exponential. Not only does it mean that you can answer interview questions more easily, but it also builds up your self-esteem and allows you to confidently stride into an interview, ready to face any question that might be thrown your way.

If you want to get to this state and be well-equipped for an interview, ask a friend to help in the rehearsal with these potential interview answers. Spend some time and take a close look at the personal qualities, knowledge, experience, and skills that you possess. Think of some potential examples where you had worked to develop on these.

Chapter 4: What To Do

As stated earlier, your preparation before the interview determines your chances of getting selected at the interview

In this chapter I will tell you how to prepare and what to do before, on the day of and after the interview.

Proper preparation helps you with the below

Understand the intention with which a question is put up

Understand what the recruiter is looking for

Synthesize confidence during the interview

- Demonstrate your willingness for the job
- Present better body language
- Indicate your seriousness towards the job
- What to do before the interview
- Prepare about the company
- Research the company website
- About the company
- Tagline and meaning
- Vision, mission and value statement (if any)
- Leadership structure
- Any recent news about the company
- Share Price
- Industry in which the company operates?
- About the industry
- Signature product(use it if possible)
- Two recent press releases
- Two nearest competitors
- Prepare about the job
- Mug up the JD
- Know if the job needs travel or not?
- Know who will be your reporting manager
- Know three things you like and dislike about the job.
- Prepare about the recruiter
- Know the recruiters name

Glance the recruiter's facebook profile
Glance the recruiter's linkedin profile
internalize the preparation template
It is imperative that you write down the answers to the questions provided in the preparation templates. If you succeed in writing all the answers in the preparation templates you are half way there. You will have the confidence to face any recruiter or number of recruiters.

I have designed the template in such a way that it provides only the necessary information but will not overload you a lot of irrelevant information.

DOCUMENTATION

Make sure to have at least three copies each of your resume, other identity verification documents and passport size photographs.

SLEEP WELL

Make sure to sleep well. A night before the interview, a sound 5 hours of sleep will help you the most to stay physical and mentally alert for the interview day

What to do on the day of the interview

Have heavy breakfast (avoid street side food for obvious reasons)

Be prepared to create the big first impression.

Avoid strenuous workouts

Arrive early

What to do after the interview

Thank the recruiter

As a general rule the process is over. Make sure to send a brief thank you note to all the recruiters. It matters a lot to a recruiter. While sending the thank you note, please consider the below

The shorter the better

Strictly refrain from asking any questions about the results

Strictly refrain from being personal. One gentle man sent me a thank you note asking if I could meet him over a cup of coffee. I replied **"Why not? But not in the next thirty days"**

Something like the below works well

Dear Mr XYZ,

I would like to extend a sincere thanks to you for giving me an opportunity of being interviewed for sales associate profile. I would also like to thank other recruiters, office administration and support staff.

You can ask for updates in exceptional circumstances. It is advised you seek guidance before asking for updates as recruiters often decline candidature of those candidates which were on hold as asking updates indicates desperation for the job.

Chapter 5: The Essentials Of A Star Behavioral Interview

Behavioral job interviews are currently considered by so many companies. The interview questions will want a persuasive illustration of your skills and experiences that are concerning the position you wish to, unlike the traditional job interview questions that will only ask you to talk about what you did in character or to share your experiences. You should be able to note that questions will be generally formatted by bringing forth a situation inquiring about what step you have taken to respond to something similar previously and what was the result.

The interviewer will ask you how you will handle a situation, and you will have to answer with a clarification of what you did. The main idea of this is to show your success previously has some positive impact on your success forthcoming. You possibly don't need to have answers in memorized in your mind, or have a sense of your experiences that you would want to share and tell about them to the interviewer.

Describe to the interviewer how you have been working effectively under pressure

The interviewer considering giving you a highly stressful job, they will want to know how good you are working under pressure. You should be able to bring out real examples that show your previous experiences with stress and how you handled the situation.

How you handle challenges and an example

Despite your job, there may be issues, and it may not turn out to be business as usual. When such questions come up, the person doing the interview will want you to tell them how you will react when you experience such awkward moments. You should have a focus on how you solved a thought-provoking condition when you respond.

Do you ever make mistakes, and how do you handle them?

There is no one perfect, and all of us will make a mistake or two at some point. The hiring manager will want to know how you took the situation when you made a mistake.

Describe how you set your objectives

The interviewer is much interested in how you come up with your plans and set the goals that you will want to execute. You can quickly get through this by giving out examples that you have experienced or have seen about successful goal setting.

Talk about the goals that you have accomplished and how you did it

The interviewer will have an interest in getting to know what you do for you to achieve your goals and which steps do you take for you to execute them.

Instances of how you worked on a team

A lot of jobs will want you to work as part of a team. An interviewer or the hiring manager will want to know how well to carry yourself when with others and how you cooperate with the other team members around you and the people you work with.

What Makes A Behavioral Interview Valid?
The most known interview queries that you will always come through are the behavioral questions. You will always come through such kinds of questions anytime you get into an interview despite what type of industry you discuss with. You should be able to know how you handle them and know what they entail. Here are some of the things that can assist you to go through. There are some elements of a STAR concept, as discussed below.

Situation

This, as the first component, will want you to know about the context of your response. You are supposed to use this component as the primary basis to expound details of the kinds of situations that you want to talk more about.

Task

This your second component in the STAR method, and it will involve the impact that you had in that environment. This component will not want to look at what you did, but it wants to look at what is expected in this situation.

Action

You have to move on to the next step by describing the activities you have by beginning to solve the situation. This component will put its focus on specific actions and the reasons why you took the actions. It is all about what happened in the real sense and not what should have been happening.

Result

This is the last component of the STAR method, and it will want to know the outcome of the aspect of everything generally. It will put all its focus on the finer details of the issue and try to understand the actions in the past components that brought about this particular outcome.

Common Behavioral Interview Questions

In cases where you have a group of individuals working towards a specific mission common amongst them in your workplace, as an employer, you will want to know how the employees will react to various circumstances. As a good employee, it is not all about being gifted to perform a role technically, but you should also be able to handle the situations that will come along with the task. Below are some of the common behavioral questions:

- You will have to talk about times when you worked closely with an individual whose personality was different from yours.
- You will be expected to talk about a situation that you wish to have handled differently with your colleague.
- You are supposed to give an example on times when you didn't meet your clients' anticipation. What happened, and what was your attempt to correct the situation?
- What are your priorities?
- Can you be able to talk about the times that you failed or succeeded? How was your reaction to the situation?
- What was your greatest achievement?
- What are the ways that help you to motivate yourself?

- Have you been able to face any conflict, what did you do?
- Are you able to give an example of a time that you tried to persuade someone?
- How do you go about your responsibilities?

Behavioral questions that you are asked will bring about some core things like:

- Ways that you can handle certain situations
- Your thinking capabilities
- Your comparison with other candidates

Such elements will give room for the interviewer to understand you deeply as a candidate. The questions will move deeper into your personality and talent that you will bring along to the workplace and what technical abilities you have to perform the role you have been given. The hiring manager will want to know about some of the things about your character when they ask you about behavioral questions. At first, they will want to see how you used to behave previously in real-world occasions. This will be very vital because the questions are not all about imagination situations, the hiring manager doesn't want to know how they will behave, but all they want to know is how you behaved.

Secondly, the questions want to know and understand the values that you have been able to add to the real situation. The person conducting the interview will want to see what you did and what are some of the expectations that made you influence the outcome. This is not all about what someone did, a group or organization did, or something that someone else presents there did, it wants to know your actions and characters and how they have an impact on the situation. The hiring manager will want to know about your activities and styles and what are the activities that you took to impress the condition.

Finally, the hiring manager will want to know how you will define and analyze various workplace conditions. This will give them a platform to have a comparison between you and the other candidates and assist them in analyzing your capability that fits to work environment.

This means you should be able to define things like success, failure, and mistake. A hiring manager is not looking for you to tell them about the real steps and the actions that you settled on. The interests they have are seeing the kind of situation you will describe to be a trial. Many people will consider unique workplace circumstances as a trial.

Steps on How to Prepare for Behavioral Questions Using The STAR

There are ways that you can begin using STAR, and it will be to your advantage, and you can get its grasp by:

- Knowing the concept of the STAR
- Reasons why you are being asked behavioral queries
- Ways in which STAR will assist you to respond to the queries

Some easy steps will help you to prepare for behavioral questions with STAR

Have a list of your skills and experiences

You should begin by first having a list of your skills and experiences. These will help you to have a good and essential performance and the role that you have succeeded after applying for it. It is not just about listing skills and the qualifications that you have, and this is because you have a lot of them. The main thing is for you to have focus on the core skills that you want for a specific particular role. For you to find out what they are, then you have to look at the job listing. You have to able to read it, underline any skill and experiences that have been mentioned by the employer and note them down in a chart. You can list many or few as they are wanted. The main point is to get the core skills behaviors that will assist you in the role and detailed task environment. You can also put into consideration other skills that the employer has not mentioned, but you know they can be of help. They can be closely related to the skills the employer said and what you have.

Choose a situation where you showcased the ability or experience

For now, you have the skills listed down. By this time, you are aware of what the employer wants and the skills your answers should have an impact on, and you have to show the skills in action. The next move you are making is about matching every talent with an actual life example. You have to get the SITUATION in STAR. You are encouraged to choose on what you have done, dealt with at some point, and you have been able to accomplish. You have to give context to your skills and appearances. It can be better when you provide examples of the situation the same as the one that you want to deal with in the new role.

Note down the STAR functions

At this point, you have to bring out your STAR template and read through every example and giving them a STAR treatment. Some templates can assist you in filling vital points that you come along. The questions in the models can be a guide when you want to write an answer. When you get to this point, then you can inscribe something close to an oral answer that you can give. You are allowed to have sample questions that are common behavioral queries with your responses.

What you have to know is how to highlight your skills and use actual examples as your responses, and you have to master the STAR strategy.

There are a few examples of behavioral job interview questions and STAR answers. For you to have the best experience, then you have to get some ideas on how to look at some examples. Some core behavioral queries are mostly unanimously asked when in job interviews. You can get to know about instances of answers or responses to the questions that have been highlighted by the STAR strategy. You are supposed to talk about the time that you were a leader and what you did. Have you ever been in a position to make a mistake? How were you able to work on it? Tell the hiring manager about an example of a goal that you have executed and how you were able to make it successful.

When you can use the STAR strategy, then you will be able to be the star of the job interview that you have gone through. Behavioral queries will assist you because they are a very vital part of the job interview. They will be used to asses you very carefully, and you will be able to analyze your fit in the company. They can tell the hiring manager who you are and the things that you have done to make some predictions about your experience in the role. When you want to answer the questions, then the best method to use will be the STAR technique. It will assist in highlighting the right elements of your past performance and will give your responses the right kind of structure and level of a feature.

The best way for you to respond to behavioral questions is by using the STAR technique. This can be a structured way you will be forming an answer. STAR also stands for Situation, Task, Action, Result. STAR matrix is a strange way that you can use for you to prepare for interviews and how you can make it possible for it to be downloaded as part of this tutorial. When you want to be successful with the behavioral-based interview, then you have to prepare well. What will kill the features of the STAR matrix is that it will force you to think more about your experiences. When you complete the matrix, then you put the skills in your short-term memory. When you come across the behavioral-based questions, then you will have an answer ready for the interviewer.

Some suggestions can help you use the STAR matrix as follows:

Situations

It can be your first job, and you don't have to worry because everyone else as somewhere to begin with. The conditions that you have should not draw anything upon your career. In cases where you are to choose a situation, then you will have to use a variety when it's possible. When you are still new in the career, then you can likely involve a combination of stories from your job, school experience, and freestyle tasks.

Tasks

You should keep your chores short and sweet. Generally, you will have to know it's your role in the situation and how the character started to be your problem or the position, to begin with.

Actions

These are the steps that you ought to take in a situation. Your potential employer will have their focus on how you handle stressful cases that you come across. What are the steps that you have taken to solve it? There are some traits that employers will use in judging potential employees:

- **Initiative** – How will potential employees find out that there is a problem to start with?

- **Approach** – What is the plan you have in solving a problem? Are you able to make decisions on how to handle things immediately, or you have to gather opinions and information on how to move on?

- **Goal-Setting** – When you begin taking actions, are you thinking what the outcome will look like?

When you are talking about your actions, be sure about putting your best foot ahead. You should have in mind what you want; someone will feel like working with you or for you.

Results

These are a very vital part of the STAR framework. You can decide to frame the perfect situation and try to describe how smooth your actions are, and it will matter if a won't focus on the outcomes. You should be able to frame the results that you had gained against the situation when you started. Some tips assist in conveying your achievements during an interview.

- You can put your results in terms of financial impact in cases where you are in a revenue-driving part of a business-like sales. You should concentrate on income created, businesses that have been won, and the future value of the clients that you added.
- Concentrate on the time savings that will have an impact on the team in cases where you have implemented a new report or analysis.

You should always have in mind that your main objective is to show a track record of success for the hiring manager to give you the job. You should link the previous achievements to the questions that you are having at hand. In mind, you should remember that having success in an interview is not the luck of the draw. When you are willing to follow all the steps of finishing the STAR matrix and have a review of your responses, then you will possibly be successful in behavioral interview occasions. There are some significant takeaways when you want to prepare for a behavioral interview, such as:

● A lot of companies tend to use a behavioral interview to assist them in getting to know how employees with capability will be able to handle conditions.

● When you follow the STAR framework on occasions when you are answering queries will assist in having your responses concise and frame how you will be able to work on situations.

● You should know that it is essential to finish the STAR matrix for you to place your matrix responses in short term memory and craft the narrative that your forthcoming boss should be able to know.

Some tutorials can help you to prepare for an interview when you read or go through them. They are as follows:

- You should look at the tutorials and business instructor on the web that has excellent tutorials on how you can be able to respond to complicated behavioral queries. You have the option of putting them in the STAR matrix, and you will see it out for them.
- There is also a good journal on how you can respond to the most common twenty interview queries.

Chapter 6: Nailing The Interview

As you wake up to the alarm which signals the time has come to prove how worthy you are, embrace the butterflies that come with acknowledging your interview is today. In fact, embrace everything about the day. You've put in all the hard work to get to this interview and be ready for it, so now relax and go through your morning routine. The most important thing now is to ensure you're in a positive, confident mental state. If there's sufficient time, exercise for half an hour before breakfast. This will help to release any stress/nerves you're harboring and to put you in a positive mood.

Also try to visualize yourself in the interview. Imagine yourself entering the room confidently and nailing each and every question; even imagine being offered the job. Visualization can really help to increase your confidence as you convince your brain that this *is* the way the interview is going to go and you *will* be successful. Even try repeating this to yourself for just five minutes before you walk out the door, "I will be successful" or "I will nail this interview". If you do this with enough conviction I can guarantee that you'll convince yourself that your success will become a reality, and your mental state will improve significantly.

The first quality employers look for in an applicant can be demonstrated before the interview even takes place: punctuality. Being on time to the interview doesn't mean walking into the building five seconds before the scheduled time. Aim to be there 15 - 20 minutes ahead of time. This will both demonstrate reliability and give yourself a chance to steady yourself. As you've already planned out how to get to the interview the previous night, avoiding being late shouldn't be a problem. Arriving early will also ensure you aren't puffing and sweating from running the last four blocks to make it on time, and will give you a chance to go to the bathroom (asking midway through an interview to use the bathroom will reflect very badly upon you).

If upon arrival you are greeted by a receptionist and asked to wait, greet them back with a smile and start a small conversation. This will help to keep your nerves at bay and maintain your positive state, and may even play a direct part in your assessment, as employers will sometimes ask the receptionist for their opinions of the applicants.

When it is time for the interview, don't allow your mood to change, keep a smile on your face the entire time while greeted by the interviewer. It takes six follow up impressions to mitigate the damage done by a bad first impression, so it's crucial to create a positive first impression and break the ice. Don't go to the length of practicing walking into the interview room and shaking the interviewer's hand, as you'll likely over think things and mess it up anyway, but just focus on being calm, positive and receptive to their questions from the moment you walk over the threshold.

If possible, try to break the ice with a light-hearted, positive comment. Something like "this office is amazing", "the weather is fantastic today" or "traffic was a breeze" provides a preliminary topic of conversation and takes the edge off as you become acquainted.Now it's time to shine! Maintain your positive energy throughout the entire interview, as well as firm, confident body language, eye contact and use of your hands to assist your explanations. When not talking keep your hands clasped together in front of you and a rigid body line, looking directly into the eyes of the interviewer. This positioning will demonstrate that you are giving them your utmost attention.

If you begin to find it difficult to concentrate and listen for whatever reason, two tactics I personally use are to scrunch your toes beneath the table, bringing your conscience mind back to the situation at hand, and switching between looking at the interviewer's left and right eye. When speaking yourself, if you lose your train of thought and forget where your answer was leading, you'd be amazed how helpful exaggerated hand movements can be to stimulate your mind in the right direction (just don't start waving your hands in the air).

When answering each of the interviewer's questions, don't lie. Answer honestly and always try to relate a past experience back to how it demonstrates your capabilities of the job at hand. You can relate almost any past experience to the job you're applying for if you're creative enough. If you're asked what experience you've had in an office team situation, you can speak about a group project you once participated in at school, or jury duty a couple of months back. If you're going for a nursing position at a local hospital and asked if you can handle working long hours, draw on a past experience of working for long hours on university assignments.

Ultimately everything on your resume should complement the position you're applying for, so you don't get any nasty shocks or are at a loss for words when the interviewer asks how your experience working at McDonald's will help with your interior designing in the future. If you're asked a question that you simply don't know the answer to at all, don't try to babble your way through it, respond with "I don't know, but I promise you that I'll find out". This shows your commitment to learning and that you'll be dedicated to being the best you can be in future.

When responding to questions, be direct. Don't use *every* question as an excuse to emphasize your best qualities. While it is important to do this, you have to judge whether each question is open ended or closed. An open ended question is something like "what experience do you have in this area?" while a closed question may be "where did you study?" Only open questions allow you to elaborate and direct the conversation where you want it to go.

A common mistake many people make is to spend too long answering each question, just begging the interviewer to abruptly cut them off with the next one. Allow yourself only one to two minutes to answer each question. End your explanation confidently and ensure you've fully covered what the question was asking in this time constraint. This helps the interview run smoothly and demonstrates that you are efficient with your time (efficient workers are better than hard workers).

Throughout the interview you shouldn't just sit there coughing out answers either. Be engaged in the flow of conversation by asking your own questions. Employers want to see that you're interested in both the company and your own future, so inquiring about what characterizes the most successful employees in the company, what opportunities exist to progress upward, what challenges the company is currently facing and what challenges new employees will typically experience. This last question will suggest that you want to ensure you'll be ready to tackle such obstacles when hired.

Aim to ask at least five solid questions throughout the interview, but no more than ten. Mentally count each one out until you've reached your goal, because once you hit it you'll be looking much more attentive and professional to your interviewer.

You now know what direct actions to take throughout the interview and how to behave, but there are still a few things that you should avoid. If you're not aware of the salary conditions already, avoid asking about this too early in the interview, but it's perfectly acceptable to ask once some rapport has been developed. Avoid all personal questions. This goes for both asking and answering them. You shouldn't be asking your future employer what their pet's name is (just yet) or how much they make a year after tax.

If a personal question is asked of you that you're not comfortable answering, politely let your interviewer know and they'll understand. Also be sure to avoid any fidgeting and negative body language.

Remember; act positive and confident, but not so cocky that you lean back with your hands behind your head, as if you've got the job already.

I should mention at this point that whilst the previous advice will seem specific to a face-to-face interview, the same etiquette is transferable for phone, video and group interviews. There are a few extra things you should focus on if participating in these interview formats, which I'll state for you now.

If you are partaking in a phone interview, ensure that you have a clear line and focus on speaking slowly so that the interviewer can understand you. Mumbling or speaking too fast is detrimental in any interview, but when the interviewer can't follow your body language or use lip-reading as a guide it is even more crucial to avoid these bad habits.

For an online video interview, test that your internet connection is reliable and create a respectable backdrop (the plainer the better as it is less distracting for the interviewer). Try to use common sense; don't have your poster of Black Sabbath or Spice Girls on the wall behind you, as you may lose some points (unless they are a fan).

In group interview situations it's even more important to be confident and make your presence felt. Don't answer every question, but even if you know only a little about a topic question, use it to demonstrate your enthusiasm. If another applicant puts forward and answer that you disagree with, raise an objection. If you can justify exactly why you disagree with another applicant's reasoning, it will go a long way to proving that you are the superior choice for the role.

In some circumstances you may be interviewed in person by several interviewers at the same time. While this will seem more intimidating, remember, the same rules apply. Only one of them can be asking a question at any one time, so focus your attention to them while they're doing this. When responding you'll want to primarily address the interviewer who asked the question, but also acknowledge the others present with your response, because they want to hear the answer as well. The key in these situations is to keep calm.

Ideally you'll know ahead of time if you will be interviewed by more than one person, but if you expect it as a possibility it shouldn't put you off guard too much when they spring it upon you. You'll be able to walk in, head held high, and greet them all with the same integrity and positivity you should have in any interviewing situation. Be glad if this is the case, because you know that you'll be better mentally prepared than the other applicants who are likely to crumble under the pressure of a panel interview, whereas you will nail it.

Chapter 7: 10 Toughest Job Interview Questions

Why did you resign from the previous job?
Tips: You can answer this question in a number of ways. You can be honest and say that the previous job was not according to your skills or there were not many opportunities in your last working position. If there is some other reason you can also state that. It is better if you have an answer that is original than the typical ones as they are easily caught.

Answer: I resigned because there were not many chances of professional growth in my previous working position and I also decided to change my career path. Since I was not finding enough time to search for proper jobs, I decided to resign and then carry on with my job hunt.

Why were you fired from the previous job?
Tips: You have to be honest but short. Nobody wants to hear about your sentiments but how you are dealing with

this difficult situation and what you have to say. Anything said in a negative air would end any chances that you may have.

Answer: I became a victim of downsizing of which I am not sure why, but all I can say is, this gave me an opportunity to look for other better opportunities and here I am, looking at amazing new prospects that have the potential of professional growth.

Which three words best describe you?

Tips: Do your homework before coming to the interview so that you are able to jot down the best words that describe you in relevance to your job. You can answer this question with great ease only if you had prepared for this at home.

Answer: I would say I am a good team player with a nice, amicable attitude. I am very detail oriented and can attentively focus on minor details most accurately.

Do you work for money or job satisfaction?

Tips: Another tricky question. You cannot say that money is not important as it will trigger a whole new discussion which you will want to avoid in any case. Job should be your first priority always. Try answering this more tactfully like the sample given below.

Answer: As they say money follows you if you work with passion, so I always go for job satisfaction. A job well done is my first priority but I will not say money is not important.

If this job does not fulfill your expectations, what will you do?

Tips: Will you leave us for something better? This question is to assess your loyalty and passion towards the job and the company. You have to prove that you will stay with reason so that it makes some sense to the interviewer.

Answer: I chose this job according to what I expect in terms of work, environment and work post. I believe that my expectations will be met and even if they do not entirely, I assure you that I am flexible enough to adapt easily.

What will you do if one of your colleagues is not actually doing his work properly and is cheating the boss?

Tips: This is not an open invitation to bad mouth your colleagues. Again this question judges how wisely you deal and answer this. You can show that you could be responsible as well as a good team player. You can narrate an incident if there is any.

Answer: I shall go to that colleague and tell him politely how his lack of attention to his work is affecting the overall quality of the entire team. I am sure this will help.

When did you last fail in something? What did you do about it?

Tips: This is one of the most favorite questions to trap the interviewee. You should be prepared to answer this question. Try telling an incident when something did not go as planned and then what you learnt from it. Do not blame anybody. This will send negative vibes that can damage your impression on the interviewer.

Answer: When I was newly hired, I was assigned the role of blah blah. My performance did not satisfy my boss as he appreciated everyone else. I went to him and asked how could I raise the standard of my work and he let me know what went wrong with my performance. I learnt that I should discuss things more often with my boss before giving him the final version.

How long can you stay with us?

Tips: Committing to some timeline is not recommended. Your answer should be more diplomatic and rounded. You should be able to continue working for the company as long as it takes to help you learn and grow as a professional. You would want to work for the company and gain experience in your field. You would want to learn all about the organization and its functions so that you can add value to your contributions towards it.

Answer: I would love to work for XYZ and polish my professional experience by working with the masters of the trade working for this organization. I would find myself fortunate if I get to work for XYZ and would continue working for as long as my contributions can add something of value.

If you were the interviewer, how would you rate yourself on a scale of 1 to 10?

Tips: Rating badly shows lack of confidence in oneself and would diminish your chances of getting the job. Rating a 100% would mean you are unthinkably, incredibly awesome and you will raise unnecessary criticism against you. The best way is to remain somewhere between 8 and 9.

Answer: I would say a 9, as my professional qualifications and education are most relevant to this job. Furthermore my work experience has groomed me in to a confident, capable and efficient hard worker but still I believe that nothing is perfect and that there is always a room for improvement.

How would you define success?

Tips: This answer depends on your goals and ambition. How far do you see yourself? Undoubtedly success is the topmost step of a ladder but then it varies from person to person as in how many and what steps they consider. Try answering this more tactfully.

Answer: Success to me is when you do your job to your own satisfaction and you get a similar response from the employer as well. For me success is what makes me happy, and a job done well, a task performed excellently is the true definition of success professionally.

Chapter 8: First Impressions

Do First Impressions Count?
Oh Yes They Do! You would be very stunned at what can be discovered from the first few moments in someone's presence. An interviewer or employer will discern a great deal about you in a relatively short time by use of their experience in body language. It's a bit like when you make new friends, generally speaking you know within a few moments of meeting a person for the very first time whether you will like them or not - despite knowing very little about their background.

This is some form of chemistry what people call instinct. So the first few seconds are fairly critical when you walk into that interview room or are greeted by the potential employer. We all give out different signals and these can be influenced by the way you dress to your body language.

In my opinion good body language starts with:

A firm handshake (Good grip) and an accompanying smile,

Being smartly dressed. Don't bathe in perfume or aftershave as strong smells often give off an overpowering smell and can be a put off. Not everyone has the same taste in cologne and there is nothing worse than being stuck in a room with a smell that makes you feel ill. It's always best to be clean and middle-of-the-road!

Before Attending Your Job Interview

It's always a good idea and a courteous one which shows initiative to confirm with your prospective interviewer the interview arrangements by phone once you have been invited to attend the interview. This doesn't need to be a long phone call. Just be brief confirming the time and place of the interview. It also gives you the opportunity to send in any documents that the interviewer may wish to see in advance or anything you may have omitted to send when you originally enclosed your CV and job application form.

Dress Code - What Clothes Should You Wear For Your Job Interview?

It's always a tough call when trying to decide what to wear for a job interview. Traditionally men always wore their smartest suit and tie and the same could be said for women – either a nice skirt and blouse or a suit. However things have changed a lot since the old days, for example if you are going to work for an IT firm or Graphic Designers then the dress code may be smart but casual - by the same token if you are going to work for a firm of Lawyers, Accountants or Insurance Brokers then the chances are the dress code is going to be formal so it can be a hard call to decide what to wear for your interview. If you are applying for an internal job then this won't apply to you as you will already know what standard of outfit is or isn't acceptable at your place of work. There are two fairly simple ways to ascertain what type of dress code your potential future employer demands and these are as follows:

Drive up to the offices or workplace at a time when the staff will be arriving or leaving – this will give you a good sign of what types of clothes the other employees are wearing.

Pick up the phone and ring up the interviewers' secretary and ask her what is the typical dress code of the company – as previously mentioned secretaries generally speaking are always keen to offer assistance to the "newbie's"!

As an indicator it's always a good idea to "Dress Above The Rest" to an interview – remember you are out to make a special impression. So a pretty simple rule - if the companies dress code is casual then you need to be dressed casually but a little smarter, for example if the other employees are wearing trousers and open neck shirts then it would be a good idea for you to wear trousers, a tie and a smart jacket. If the dress code is a suit and tie then you need to wear your best suit and tie – get the picture it's pretty easy for you to judge for yourself.

Another good idea to point out is that when you are invited into the interview; don't ever remove your jacket without being asked. If the room is hot – well quite frankly that's just a bit of tough luck. Reason being that we all perspire during stress and there is nothing as bad as seeing perspiration marks around the arms of your shirt! So what type of clothes should you wear at your interview? Well it's an individual's choice really.

However steer well clear of bright outrageous ties if you are a man as not every interviewer will share your love of bright colors - try and settle on neutral colors. Taking the middle ground approach on what colors to wear, will not attract unnecessary attention to you....Remember in the end what really matters is the content and not the container!

Finally as previously mentioned it's a bad idea to wear overpowering aftershave or perfume – it can put off others.

Your Arrival At The Job Interview

Any organized person will strive to arrive at any interview in good time. This should give you a few moments to compose yourself and utilise the rest room before your big moment. If at the office there are some bathrooms in the waiting area go and make a few final checks on your appearance. You might want to comb your hair, use the lavatory or adjust your make up if you are a lady.

This little time will give you the opportunity to make sure that you are looking great, it will also give you reassurance so that once you are in the interview you don't have to worry about whether you have done your zips up or whether your hair looks tidy — issues that are important but that you don't want to have to worry whilst trying to win over the interviewer.

It's always a good idea if you have a briefcase and if wearing a tie to take a spare just in case you spill something on it before going into the interview. It can easily happen to anyone.

When You Are Called Into The Interview Room

This is the time when you are entering the unfamiliar territory – new ambiance, new faces - sometimes as many as six or a strange room. You need maximum focus at this point as "First Impressions" do count. So how do you greet your interviewer? Firstly look your interviewer in the eyes and smile; everyone likes a smiley face - just a pleasant friendly smile.

Secondly, offer out your hand for a hand shake - remember don't squeeze the interviewers hand just to show that you lift weights (just a firm professional handshake will do) and offer an accompanying greeting ("Hello very pleased to meet you Sir/Madam" or something like that).

Your interviewer will then either take you into the interview room (or you may already be in there as you have been called in) and offer you a seat. Please do not just sit down when you enter the room, wait to be offered a seat – its good manners.

The interview is going to start along the lines of chit chat to put you at ease, you will probably be asked how your journey was and probably offered a drink. Depending on the type of person you are and how well you cope with nerves (and remember we all have them, from the person applying for a job cashier in a restaurant to the executive applying for a 500K plus per month position) it's up to you whether you decide to accept a drink. You won't be thought of any less should you not accept a drink - and if you think your hands are going to be shaking like a tree in a typhoon every time you pick your cup up - it's probably a good idea to decline. That way you won't chance spilling the liquid all down your front.

Chapter 9: Dressing For The Interview

Your image plays a major role in your first impression, believe it or not. As simple as it sounds, I've seen candidates who have chosen to ignore this advice and others who cut corners thinking they could get away with it. Whether you're interviewing for an entry level position at a fast food chain or for a management position with a financial institution, the dress code remains the same.

Let's take a look at it from the other side of the table. If 2 candidates walked in for an interview, one dressed in a well fitted suit and the other dressed casually, whom would you choose to represent the company based on image alone? The candidate being hired is a direct reflection of the hiring manager's decision. The hiring manager will not hire anyone that will potentially make him or her look bad as a decision maker. Let's take a look at how you should dress and what you should avoid.

For Men

Suit up. Your business attire needs to include a suit (matching jacket and dress pants), shirt, tie, belt, dress socks, and dress shoes.

Suit – Keep it conservative. Dark colored suit with a light colored shirt. Remember, if your suit is a dark color, your shirt should be a light color, and vice versa. A solid black suit is great, but a solid navy blue or solid grey suit works as well.

Shirt - As for your shirt, solid white is fine, but don't be afraid to wear a shirt with pinstripes or patterns. Just make sure it is minimal. If the design or colors seem like a distraction, or even if you question it multiple times, then it's best to play it safe and look at other options. Your shirt should always be tucked in.

Tie – The color of your tie should compliment your shirt. Keep the pattern minimal or go with a solid color if your shirt has minimal patterns. Avoid ties with cartoon characters or other images. When you wear your tie, it should reach the top of your belt.

Watch, belt, socks, and shoes – Wear a watch that compliments your suit. It shows the interviewer that you know how to manage your time. Jokes aside, keep it simple yet elegant. Do not wear athletic or casual watches. Keep it dressy. A black or brown colored dress belt will look great with any suit. Belts should always be worn, regardless if it's needed to hold up your pants or not. The color of your socks should coordinate with your suit. Wear dress socks, not athletic socks. Dress socks reach halfway up your calf. Athletic socks are easily noticed when you are seated. A pair of black lace-up shoes is versatile and works with almost any suit.

Fitting – It's more important than the cost of the attire. Know your measurements or visit a store to get measured if needed. Shirts are measured by neck size and arm length. You should be able to comfortably fit one finger between the collar of your shirt and your neck. Also pay attention to the fit of the shirt. They come in slim fit, fitted, and regular. Your shirt should closely fit your torso. Avoid long length suits. Your pants should have little break at the ankle to where it just touches the top of your shoes.

For Women

While women's business attire isn't as simple as men's, the best way to approach each decision is keep it conservative. This should be remembered for everything, from tops to bottoms, jewelry, makeup, and perfume.

Suit – A suit with a skirt bottom or pant is recommended. When in doubt of which to choose, make the conservative decision. When wearing a skirt, make sure the length is no shorter than the end of your fingers when your arms extend at your sides. Under the suit, wear a cotton or silk blouse with a collar in a neutral color. Avoid sleeveless tops, spaghetti straps, casual sweaters, and t-shirts.

Fitting – This is one of the most important decisions to make when it comes to your entire business attire. Interviewers will notice the length of your skirt. If you choose to wear a skirt, make sure it is at knee length. Your top should not be low cut, lacy, or sheer. Avoid anything that may seem to be a distraction. Make sure your clothes aren't too tight fitted. Make proper alterations to your attire if needed.

Makeup and Nail Polish – Keep your makeup simple and the colors should be neutral to your skin tone. Avoid long nails and colors that can be flashy or distracting.

Jewelry – Jewelry should be minimal. Wear no more than a single ring per hand. Earrings should not be too long and avoid oversized hoops. If your jewelry is constantly jingling, then that's a sign that it shouldn't be worn. Avoid shiny, flashy, and distracting jewelry. If you normally wear nose rings, multiple earrings, or piercings, leave them at home.

Bag/Purse – A tote bag is ideal for interviews. It should be large enough to carry your business portfolio and additional material needed for the interview. If you choose to carry a purse along with a tote bag, keep it small so it isn't a hassle when you're carrying two bags at once.

Shoes – Flats, heels, and dress boots are fine as long as they are not open toe or open back. If you're going to wear heels, it is better to wear low heels. Choose a color that compliments your suit and bag. Avoid sandals, high boots, and athletic shoes.

Nails – Trim your nails, make sure they're clean, and get a manicure. Interviewers notice nails that are uncared for. Avoid colors/designs that may be a distraction.

Final Tips for Men and Women

Your business attire should be clean, neat, and well pressed. If you're going to use cologne or perfume, less is better than more. Keep the jewelry minimal. You shouldn't be wearing anything more than a watch, wedding ring, and earrings (for women). Men, make sure your beard and mustache are trimmed, if not shaved.

Investing time in preparing your business attire is investing time in your first impression. A good friend/hiring manager once told me, "I spend as much time interviewing as they spend preparing for the interview". Hiring managers notice all of the details during the interview. Invest time in yourself, so they feel confident in investing their time with you.

Chapter 10: Maintaining Motivation

You can't depend on outside forces to keep you motivated. You have to motivate yourself by doing simple things in order to be more productive. You have to reserve your energies for bigger issues which may affect you later.

Take short breaks every hour. If you're very focused on your work, you'll surely feel tired or monotonous. This is why you have to rest even for just 10 minutes. However, you have to ensure that you use these mini breaks wisely. You have to set a time for these short breaks and be disciplined enough to stick to it.

If you want to maintain your motivation while you work, you can just look at what you accomplished while working. It's good to have a to-do list which you can tick off when you accomplish a task. It inspires you to get going. Also, if you're fond of reading, you can read interesting articles about motivation. If you're in the office, you can have a cup of coffee in the pantry.

A quick chat with an officemate can be a good diversion. However, you mustn't get distracted from your real tasks at hand. You can even just clear your office table. If your table is really messy, you can organize it just to clear your mind.

If you notice most people, they are committed to get the job done. They may not do it perfectly but they do their best. If you want to get better results, commit to do everything well. This way, you also gain personal motivation, self image, and self respect. You must strive for excellence but not necessarily in a perfect manner. You have to remind yourself everyday that you're not perfect but you do have your own strong points. Every morning, you can write all your strong attributes on a piece of paper so you'll gain a powerful sense of yourself. This will dramatically increase your motivation.

For some people, it may be difficult to see themselves as somebody successful. However, there are also people see themselves as successful in the future yet they don't make it a habit to work really hard everyday. This is where the conflict in self image lies. You have to see yourself as unstoppable so that when you're faced with inevitable obstacles you remain effective and positive. You can write "unstoppable" on a notepad then stick it to a place where you'll see it everyday.

Highly ambitious people keep on focusing on those things that they have yet to accomplish. They don't congratulate themselves for every achievement they have. Over time, they lose their motivation to move forward. If you remind yourself every day of the achievements you did for the day, you'll feel good about yourself and remain motivated. You can even list them down before you go to sleep.

How To Keep Your Spirits High

You have to have short-term and long-term goals so that you remain focused on achieving them. You stay motivated every time you check your progress. You can set weekly benchmarks so that you'll know if you're progressing or digressing. If you find yourself behind these benchmarks, you have to kick start your motivation so that you remain on the right track.

Whenever you achieve your weekly goals, you have to reward yourself. It can be a trip to a spa, a bowl of ice cream, or dinner at your favorite restaurant. The rewards need not be expensive. They can be small mementos to remind you to keep going towards your bigger goals. It is also important to give yourself a break at times. You will feel overwhelmed if you become very determined to meet your goals. You'll surely burn yourself out.

At times, you'll feel that you've fallen short. What you can do is learn the lesson then move on. You strive to meet your weekly goals next time. You have to stay within the schedule even if you've encountered a difficulty. The strategy is to keep moving and not dwell on your failure. Lastly, you can read and watch motivational speeches or stories. These will your pep talk and will keep you inspired.

Some Interview Questions And Answers
Question: What motivates you?

Why this may be asked: The interview wants to know why you're successful in what you do. He wants to understand what you value in your work.

Possible answers: You must prepare for this question prior to going to the job interview. Critical thinking is needed for you to answer this properly. As such, you need to look at your resume and list down all the things you enjoy doing and those tasks which keep you motivated. You have to choose the tasks which are related to the job you're being interviewed for. You can also consider the work environment you know you'll excel in.

"I was assigned several projects as a director of development teams. I implemented repetitive processes and my teams were able to deliver the projects on time. I was motivated because these projects were challenging."

"The company's clients have to be provided with the best service that I can offer. I see to it that I offer a positive customer experience every time. I try to develop my customer service skills so that

I can always deliver my best performance for my company."

"I always want to meet a deadline. It brings me a great sense of accomplishment whenever I set and reach deadlines. I keep myself organized so that I can complete every task and stay within the schedule.

The job interviewer wants to understand your persistence and resilience so he asks you about motivation. He wants to know how you deal with difficult obstacles, challenges, and setbacks because you'll face all of these in every job you work on. At times, when you encounter a roadblock, it isn't intellect or skills that will make you overcome it. Your passion and attitude will determine how you'll solve a particular problem.

Chapter 11: Company And Industry Questions

What is Your Perspective on the Future of the Industry

This answer is all about homework. Understand the vision of the company for which you are applying. Most likely, you've selected this company as one where you would like to work, because it aligns with where you believe the industry should go. Be ready to articulate that and to ask questions around this to the interviewers. The wrong answer is having no answer and not having done your homework. Other than that, the interviewers are seeking to understand if your vision aligns with theirs.

Winning answer (if applying at Nordstrom's):

Overall, retail is getting more competitive. There are only so many ways to compete. I love that Nordstrom's competes not only with the highest quality brands but also in its world-renowned service. As online shopping becomes more prevalent, it seems like the Nordstrom's online experience is also among the best. Besides that, the different "tiers" to which Nordstrom's caters through the other stores is also effective. With Nordstrom's Rack, you have a middle tier client and then Last Chance caters to the bargain hunters.

Why Do You Want to Work Here?

This is another question which relies heavily on the homework you have done. It's best to know of 4 important areas: what sets the company apart from the others, knowledge of the company's history, opportunities for future growth in the company, and testimonies of people you know who work there.

Do your research: discover what sets the company apart from all the others. If your answer can be the same for this question when interviewed by a competitor company, it's not unique enough. General statements aren't enough. When you're able to tell the interviewer what you think makes the company unique and that uniqueness makes you want to work for the company, it sends the signal you're serious about joining the company, and it's not just because you want a job. This gives the message that the company can count on you to be loyal to them, and there is a likelihood you'll stay with the company for a long time. This is a quality companies appreciate.

Know about the company's significant developments and milestones. It's enough to have a few speaking points you find interesting about the company.

Identify key opportunities for future career growth with the company and by expressing your genuine excitement for such opportunities. Again, this shows you're genuinely interested in the company. It also lets the interviewer know that hiring you will be a win-win situation for you and the company, because your goals are aligned with each other.

If possible, it's also helpful to share the testimonies of people you know who worked or are working there, and how their testimonies speak to you of how exciting it must be to be part of the organization. Be specific and avoid general claims, such as "I have friends who love the millennial culture here"; instead, be specific like, "I love how the company supports its employees by sending them to very important trainings at least once a year at the company's expense."

Chapter 12: Questions You Should Ask

Near the end of the interview, you will be asked if you have any questions. This could be one of the most important aspects of your interview. Not only is it your turn to interview them, find out everything you want to know about the company and position, but also impress them with your genuine interest!

Without a doubt, the candidates who ask relevant questions always come out above the ones who don't ask questions. Below are a few great questions you should ask. You don't need to ask them all, especially since some of them might have already been discussed earlier in the interview. Just pick two or three, write them down, and bring them with you so you don't draw a blank when it's your turn to ask questions.

Questions about the position

Why is this position vacant? The answer will give you some good insight. You might learn if the position is new because of company growth, or if there was a person in this position before who left – were they promoted? Did they leave because they were unhappy?

Is there any growth or future upward mobility for this position? Basically you want to know what your career path would be if you were in this position. Can you eventually be promoted to lead, supervisor, manager, etc.? Will you learn skills to apply to other positions within the company?

Questions about the company

Does the company have any plans to go public? – Be sure they aren't already a publicly traded company before asking this. If they are a small company, don't ask this.

How would you describe the company culture? This is always an excellent question and gives you some real insight into the environment and how the employees are treated.

Does the company have any community involvement? You're looking to see if and how they support local causes and events.

Questions about the hiring timeframe

How soon are you planning to close the position? You **must ask this** if it hasn't already been discussed. You will regret it when you get home if you forgot to ask this and you have no idea when you can expect to hear from them.

After the Interview

Give thanks

Once you've left the interview be sure to follow up with a thank you. A hand written thank you card mailed to the office gives it a nice personal touch. If it's a less formal environment a simple email to thank the interviewer for their time is sufficient.

As a recruiter I received many thank you emails over the years and always forwarded them on to the hiring managers. It helps the hiring managers to keep you in the forefront of their minds and lets them know that you're still interested.

Follow up

At this point it's pretty much a waiting game. Hopefully they told when they would be closing the position and getting back to you. Hopefully you asked! Unfortunately not all employers reach out to their applicants to let them know when the position is filled. It's not very professional but it happens often when there are a high number of applicants and open positions.

A good rule of thumb is to wait 5-7 days after the interview. If you haven't heard from them, give them a call and ask about the status of the position. That is, of course, unless they've given you a time frame. If they told you it would be a month and you call after only a week, you will only make yourself look bad!

Chapter 13: How To Make The Most Of Your Resume, Even If You Are Underqualified

Sometimes it's worth pressing "apply," even if you don't quite fulfill the job description. You're dying to apply for a killer job you just found. It looks nearly perfect. But there's one tiny problem—you're under qualified.

1. Do you go for it, or let it pass on by?

It depends. And while there's no perfect answer or formula for this, here are a few instances in which you should (and shouldn't) take a run at a job that looks amazing, even it feels slightly out of reach.

2. Should: you're just a bit shy on years of experience

The job description asks for seven to 10 years of experience. You have just under six, and a little more if you count the (entirely) relevant internship you took on while finishing your degree.

Dear heavens, go for it. Now, you'll want to make sure and make it clear that you've got the knowledge, business acumen, and maturity of someone with that seven to 10 years of experience (your cover letter is a good place to strongly hint toward all these things), and you may want to include that internship (just in case they're officially doing the math), but don't let a small shortage scare you away.

3. Shouldn't: you're not even in the ballpark

Now, if you're only a year or two into your career, you may be wasting your time going after a role that requires several additional years. Is it impossible? Maybe not, but it's improbable, especially if you follow the "normal" application process of uploading your resume through an online portal. Instead, I'd consider working to uncover a similar, but maybe earlier stage opportunity at the same company or, if you are hell-bent on taking a run at it, find a direct "in" at that organization. You're going to need an opportunity to state your case directly with a human decision maker (because the resume-scanning software will more than likely rule you out).

4. Should: you lack a degree, but it doesn't say "required"

The education section of a job description is an important one to examine. Most companies are quite clear on their minimum requirements, as well as their stance on considering candidates with an equitable mix of education and experience.

If the description doesn't say the degree is a must, then it's fair to assume that the potential employer will consider a highly qualified candidate without it. Not sure?

If you can uncover a contact at the company of interest (if no one's listed on the job description, start with their talent acquisition or HR team), you may want to do something many of your competitors won't—pick up the phone and call.

(Gasp!)

"Hi. I see that you're looking for a senior project manager. The job description suggests that you are considering highly qualified candidates that do not have a bachelor's degree. Can you confirm this?" Done.

5. Shouldn't: the job description makes it clear that degree is mandatory

Some companies have hard and fast minimum degree requirements. It's hard to get around this and maybe a waste of time if you apply to a blind mailbox (or through an online portal) without that piece of paper. Also, realize that a bunch of other candidates who apply will have the degree, so when a blob of resumes comes in through the system, whose do you think will be reviewed first? That's right, the ones with the mandatory degree.

If you feel very strongly about making a case for yourself, you need to get directly to someone of influence on the inside and state your case, rather than relying on the scanning software.

6. Should: you lack a preferred credential (or two), but have almost everything else

You do realize that most job descriptions are giant wish lists, yes? Few people are going to match every single qualification.

That'd be like making a list for Santa and waking on Christmas morning to discover every last item you requested under the tree. Right. That said, as long as you're at about an 80% match to the job requirements, in most instances you should take a run at it, especially if the ones you're lacking are listed under the "preferred" section (as opposed to the "required").

7. Shouldn't: you lack a required license or certification

Now, if you're at 80% (or even 90%) yet lack a required license or certification (e.g., real estate license, registered nurse designation, lawyer who has passed the state bar, etc.), you are more than likely wasting your time. In some fields, you just simply cannot be hired without certain credentials. So your choice is to either go get those credentials or select another path.

8. Should: the job description says, "local candidates only" and you're moving to that town

When you're preparing to relocate to a new city, it's completely natural that you'll begin sleuthing out opportunities there, even if you've not yet established concrete timing for the move. If the plans are already in motion—and you're expecting to cover moving costs on your own—don't be discouraged if you come across the phrase, "local candidates only." More often than not, this is code for, "We're not funding your move," not, "If you didn't graduate from the local high school, forget about it." You'll need to make it clear in your cover letter that the move's imminent, of course, but don't let this phrase dissuade you.

9. Shouldn't: it says, "local candidates only" and you expect a relocation package

Again, this phrase is your blaring announcement that they're not paying to move someone into town for the job, probably not even if they love you. Relocations are expensive, adding an easy five figures to any new hire. If you're looking to move on a company's dime, it's probably best to steer away from job descriptions that (kindly) state "forget about it" right there in the job description. Are there exceptions to these rules? Sure, sometimes there are (outside of jobs that require certain licenses—you won't get around that one). But don't count on being the anomaly.

It will likely waste your time and theirs, and leave you feeling unnecessarily frustrated. Instead, apply for jobs that align pretty well with your background and aspirations and—when you know you'll only make sense to the decision makers if you have opportunity to explain—then find a way to get to them directly.

TIPS

Exploit your transferable skills.

Consider a chrono-functional resume.

Understand what you're stepping into.

Dig deeper than others.

Get really good recommendations.

Complete a pre-interview project.

Connect with the hiring manager.

Tell the truth.

Chapter 14: Etiquette At Job Interview

Etiquette at job interview is a very important aspect to help any candidate land a job. Apart from other important aspects of your interview, etiquette is also one of the main areas employers can use to decide whether to hire you or not. Your body language could be used to tell the kind of a person you are.

Below are excellent tips for etiquette to be utilized during your interview. With just a few small elements, you can state a lot without speaking a word.

Know your interview location and be early. Get directions beforehand and do a dry run to the location several days prior to your interview so that on the day of your interview, you can find the building easily, saving you time and stress. Getting there 10-15 minutes early shows that you are punctual, professional and prepared.

Greeting - make sure to greet your interviewer. Firstly, thank him or her for inviting you to the interview before getting started. Gratitude goes a long way!

Address the man or woman by the proper title i.e. Mr. or Mrs. If you have a woman interviewer and are unsure if she is married or not, then address her by "miss." You can also use "sir" or "ma'am" to address an interviewer unless the recruiter tells you otherwise.

Switch off your phone - This should be common sense for most people. No sounds should be heard from your phone at all during the interview. If you must use your phone for any reason i.e. you need to look up the phone number of a reference or you are searching for a form the recruiter emailed you, ask permission before doing so.

Handshake – When being introduced to the person who will interview you, it is proper to use a firm handshake. There is a proper and improper way to shake another's hand. A firm handshake with eye contact is the proper way to introduce yourself to another person. I must stress here that I have shaken many hands and notice something very disturbing, especially in women known as the "wet noodle." This is when shaking a woman's hand, she uses an extremely loose grip that only states that she is not too interested in or engaged in the interaction going on. This is the opposite of the message you are trying to send. There is nothing more unprofessional than a handshake such as this. On the other hand, which I have experienced with some men, is a handshake that is too firm, almost painful. This can be interpreted as arrogant, aggressive or controlling. Squeeze the other person's hand just enough to be firm, being sure to make strong eye contact with your interviewer, showing that you are assertive and confident.

Proper Eye Contact – Strong eye contact is essential in an interview for virtually the entire interview. If this feat seems too hard, you can look at the bridge of the interviewer's nose and s/he will not be able to tell that you are not looking into his/her eyes.

Proper Research on the Company – This point is mentioned many times in this book and we cannot stress the importance of this enough. You need to be "in the know" about the organization, from marketing strategy, to financial status, to new initiatives. Any insider information should be gained prior to the interview.

Come with Resume In Hand – Always bring a copy of your resume and cover letter to the interview in the event the recruiter does not have a copy or in the event you need to refer to it during the interview, typically for a timeline question. For example, I have held many positions throughout the years so it is helpful for me to glance at my resume to remind me of dates which I held specific positions.

Wait for the interviewer to offer you a chair - Don't just sit immediately you get into a job interview room. Don't create a scene that will make the hiring team judge you by your behavior or character. In addition, when sitting, be sure to use excellent posture by sitting at the edge of your seat, showing that you are attentive and listening. Never slouch or sit all the way back in your chair to make yourself comfortable. You are not at home! Be attentive and ready for questioning.

Refrain from smoking before your interview. Let's face it! It's stinky, unappetizing and unattractive (for most). It is best to avoid doing this until after your interview is over and you are out of sight and range of the company. Even if the interviewer offers you a cigarette, it is not advisable to smoke.

Avoid too much talking, stick to the point and allow the interviewer to control the conversation. Your main tasks should be answering questions and listening to what the hiring team has to say. Do not ask the interviewer any questions unless asked to do so or unless you first ask permission to ask a question.

Best not to use "yes" or "no" phrases. Elaborate on your answers to ensure you are truly getting to the heart of the answer to the interviewers' satisfaction. Remember you are selling yourself to the interviewer and simple answers like 'yes' or 'no' are not enough to convince him/her that you are the best fit for the job. Explain yourself as much as possible by responding to the questions in a detailed manner.

Like the topic of salary, refrain from inquiring about benefits, allowances, or vacations until after the job offer is made to you. Since perks of a job are treated similarly in theory as the topic of salary, the interviewer can deduct points from your overall interview "score" for mentioning these before an offer has been made to you. However, if your acceptance of the job is resting on benefit specifics, then you can ask about these after the job has been offered to you. There is an unspoken "window" of time after a job offer has been made that negotiating on these benefit-specifics are acceptable. Be sure that the time-off days, personal days, and vacation days are in amounts that are satisfactory to you. Otherwise, if you need some time to think about an offer, tell the recruiter that you need to discuss the details with your family, but be sure to get back to him or her within 24 hours, especially if you plan on taking the position.

Smile! Don't overdo it, but providing a warm and honest smile during your interview shows that you are a friendly person who is enthusiastic about the position and perhaps about life in general. It is a great technique to use and also shows that you have a positive attitude.

Maintain strong eye contact - Glancing confidently to the hiring team during an interview proves that you are a confident person who can take any responsibility head on. Experts recommend looking at the interviewer's eyes and not any other part. If you are being interviewed by several hiring team members, be sure to look back and forth to each person and do not get fixated on one person.

Try to use your hands to explain yourself. However, you should limit the number of gestures you make using hands. Do this in a confident way and see how effective it is when it comes to communication during an interview. Excessive hand gestures can affect you negatively on how you perform in a job interview.

Chapter 15: Remembering The Basics

Now that we have made it past preparing with the actual interview and grooming, lets go over a few topics that some people forget. These are basic things people forget right before the job interview.

Plan what to bring with you to the interview location. Make sure you have at least three copies of your resume. If you are told that your interview will be conducted by more than two people or a panel, bring enough copies of your resume to make sure everyone has a copy plus one extra resume. Bring a notepad and two black or blue ink pens. If you want to show examples of your work, make sure you take your portfolio. Have information needed to complete an application such as references and their contact information, previous school addresses, and your past employers contact information.

"Where are My Keys!" Be proactive about what may cause last minute stress and not reactive to panicking. Make sure you know the night before where your car keys are located if you have a morning interview and during morning hours if you have an afternoon interview. There is nothing more nerve rattling then not being able to find your car keys. It will also reduce the stress of calling a company to inform them that you are going to be late or not able to attend the interview because you can't find your car keys.

Print out the directions or write out the directions on the notepad that you will take with you to the interview. Even if you have the best GPS in the world, make sure you know where you are going in case something tragic happens to your GPS. Make sure you know where you are going the day before the interview. If you are driving, you want to make sure you account for traffic when calculating the time to drive to the interview. If you are going to take a bus or train to your interview, make sure you know the fastest route and plan well in advance to make sure you will know how far you will have to walk to the interview site from the bus or train stop. There are several really good phone apps that can help calculate travel times. Review your travel route before the interview day.

For heaven's sake, check to make sure you have enough gas in your vehicle to get to the interview the day before your interview. I once was waiting on someone to arrive for an interview and the person ended up being 15 minutes late to the interview. I didn't acknowledge that the person was late, but the person gladly volunteered that they were only a little late because they had to stop for gas. I couldn't believe I heard that. I was thinking that this person has just sealed their fate in a negative way regarding the outcome of how this interview will proceed. Don't put yourself in a position of being late for an interview because of a task that should have been completed before the interview time.

Check to make sure you have your pass to ride a bus or train, bus fare, train fare, or money for a ride share service. Don't leave anything to chance.

The goal is to arrive early to the interview. You don't want to enter the interview looking stressed out because you were rushing to get to the location. You may have to fill out an application or provide a copy of your resume for the interviewer to quickly review before the interview begins. If your interview is at 2:00 p.m. and you arrive at 1:59 p.m., you are not going to be seen within the next minute or even the next five minutes if you have to fill out paperwork. Being early is one way to show that you value the interviewer's time and you are on the path to confidently be considered for the job.

If you know that you will be late, call the interviewer immediately. See if it will be permitted to proceed with the interview that day or if you will be able to reschedule. Apologize for not being on time and let them know that you are available to arrive by a specific time. As an interviewer, I have understood that things happen. If the person called to let me know that they are running a few minutes late, that has not formed a completely bad impression with me. Although, if they are more than 10 minutes late without calling, then I might not be as understanding about being late. Some interviewers will cancel the interview if the person is late and definitely if the interviewee is more than 15 minutes late.

Before you walk through the door to say "hello," take the gum out of your mouth. There's nothing more distracting then a person chewing gum during an interview. The more nervous some people get, the harder they chew gum and the chances of blowing a bubble are 50/50 which is distractive to the interviewer and a sign of the interviewee being unprofessional.

Make sure you greet everyone that you make eye contact with while at the location with a smile. You never know who is who when you are at the location. Every company is different. If you are sitting in a lobby, you may not know who the people are walking back and forth from the entrance to back offices and cubicles while you wait. You could be looking directly at the person interviewing you or the big boss who signs the paychecks. You want to make a good impression and not create a memory of them remembering you as the person who sat there not willing to greet them before you were introduced. Also, some interviewers will even ask the receptionist how they viewed your demeanor. Smile, and remember to be courteous to everyone.

Chapter 16: How Much Should You Tell During The Interview?

It can be difficult to know what to say during an interview or how much information you should provide. It is very easy to provide more information than is necessary when you are anxious to be hired for a job. Some applicants make the mistake of thinking the more information they give, the better their chances are of being chosen. There is some information that just doesn't need to be provided—you only need to provide information that is pertinent to the position for which you are applying for.

How do you know what to reveal? The best rule of thumb is to only answer direct questions and only provide information that is relevant to the position for which you are applying for. If you were terminated from a previous job and the interviewer doesn't ask about it, you are under no obligation to provide that information. In most cases, the interviewer is only going to be interested in experiences that relate to the job for which you are applying, unless the position in question was your last one. In that case, do not reveal more information than what the interviewer asks. Most employers today only ask for the job title and the dates of your employment; the less you say the better. In fact, many companies are using third party agencies to provide job verifications, so most companies are not checking references like they used to do.

Many things that employers used to ask in interviews have been stopped under the discrimination law. For instance, employers are no longer allowed to ask your age or marital status during the interview. Of course, once you are hired these things will be important for insurance purposes. Employers are also not allowed to ask about children or childcare arrangements because in the past women with children were often denied employment because of concerns about not having enough time or concentration on the job because of children at home. Of course, some may still ask, but you are under no obligation to discuss your family arrangements unless they are needed for insurance purposes after you are hired. The more information you reveal the more reasons you give a prospective employer to eliminate your name from qualified applicants.

Guarantee a Successful Interview

Interviewing for a job can be one of the most difficult tasks to undergo but if you follow some simple suggestions, you will increase your chances for success. When you have a successful interview, you greatly increase your chances of being hired for the position though there is never a guarantee. However, knowing how to guarantee a successful interview is the first step—you surely will not be hired if you are unsuccessful in the interview phase. Many job seekers fail because they either don't know or do not adhere to proper interview protocol. Knowing what to do and say in an interview can help you have a more successful interview.

How you are dressed is the biggest challenge to a successful interview, especially for young applicants. Young people are not usually into the habit of wearing skirts, dresses and suits and thus do not see the need for having them just for a job interview. You will create a better impression overdressing than under dressing. Always look professional. If you do not own anything formal, at least wear business casual clothing—never casual clothing—to an interview. If you do not own any, buy one for your interview or borrow an outfit from a friend or relative.

The way you carry yourself will have a positive or negative effect on a successful interview. This is important when it comes to the way you handle yourself in the interview. One of the most important things to remember is to maintain eye contact with the interviewer. If you are looking around the room, out the window, looking down and or fidgeting, the interviewer does not know if you are focused on him or her or your mind is wandering on other things. The interviewer might also think you might have a short attention span. If the interviewer thinks your mind is elsewhere, he or she will end the interview short and you will lose any opportunity you might have had of securing a position with that company.

Make Your Interview a Success

Some people are very good at interviewing techniques while others do not have the slightest idea what to do. Interviews can be very stressful, especially for those who has never been to an interview before. The same goes to those who are out of work, soon to be out of work or just unhappy with their current position. You can ease a great deal of the stress you suffer preceding and during an interview if you know some of the important things to do in order to ensure success. That does not mean you will necessarily be the hired, but you will increase your chances and learn how to conduct yourself to achieve the highest likelihood for success.

Even though it is a common misconception for younger job seekers, your attire is very important during an interview. For those who have the idea that you should be accepted as who you are, remember also that employer does not have to hire you. With so many people unemployed today, you are a fool if you think an employer is not going to put personal appearance on the top of their list. If you do not wear professional or at least business casual dress any other time, it is essential to wear that style to an interview.

Showing the prospective employer you know something about their company, will help increase your chances of being hired for the position. It shows that you have enough interest in the company to take time to learn about its history and products or services. This will gain you points in the mind of the interviewer. In addition having someone that already knows something about the company makes it easier during the training process. If you have no idea about the company, this might cast a doubt in the interviewer's mind why you have applied in the first place. It is also time consuming for them to explain to someone who knows nothing about their company about what they do, sell or offer.

Attention and eye contact are essential when you are being interviewed. When you focus on the interviewer and what they have to say, you will also have a better chance for securing the job you are applying for. It is easy to lose a potential job when the interviewer feels that you are uninterested in what he or she has to say. Your attention is very important; you need to maintain eye contact with your interviewer at all times.

Chapter 17: Developing The Letter Of Introduction

<u>Overview</u>

By now, you have learned that the letter of introduction is your primary means of contacting prospective interviewees. As the name indicates, the letter of introduction is where you formally introduce yourself to prospective interviewees and request their permission to interview them. If you are wondering just how important this letter is, I can tell you that your ability to secure an informational interview will hinge upon how well it is written. Why? Because you are sending an unsolicited letter to someone who does not know you, and that person will be judging you based on your letter. Taking it a step further, that person will be assessing frankly, whether you are worth their time. This does not mean you have to be a Journalism or English major. It just means you will need to take your time and develop a straightforward, sincere narrative of why you would like their help, taking great care to ensure it is free of errors and that it conforms to correct standards of grammar. Think about how inclined you would be to help someone who sent you an unsolicited email with a convoluted message riddled with grammar and punctuation errors. Would you take them seriously? Chances are you wouldn't, which is why great care must be taken to ensure it sends the right message and reflects the work of some who is serious about their business.

I can tell you from experience that a well-constructed email can yield truly amazing results. I have personally used this type of email and the results have been nothing short of exceptional. This is not to say that everyone will achieve the same results, but I'm telling you flat out that, if done correctly, it can open the doors to opportunity. People are willing to help you if you ask, but your request must be executed in the appropriate manner.

Anatomy of the Letter of Introduction

The first step in constructing this email is to organize your ideas and thoughts so that you can present them in a clear, concise, and persuasive manner. The letter of introduction is not the place to tell your life's story. There is no time for that. Your letter will instead convey three simple things: (1) it will tell the reader who you are and how you found them; (2) why you want their help and what you hope to achieve; and (3) explain the nature of the interview. Keep in mind, the people you are reaching out to are busy and have no time to read **War and Peace.** One of the most important things to remember is to use as few words as possible to make your point. If your message is too lengthy, the reader will most likely delete it before they finish reading, especially coming from someone they do not know. An overly lengthy email signals to the reader that you lack an understanding of professional email etiquette. You want to ensure you make it as easy as possible on the reader in order for them to render a decision on your behalf. What you **do not** want to do is construct one behemoth email with no paragraph breaks or clear breaks in ideas. If you have ever received this kind of email then you know what I amtalking about. With that bit of information out of the way, let's now break down each part. Not unlike any other formal correspondence, the informational interview consists of your standard introduction, body, and conclusion.

> Dear Ms. Subject Matter Expert,
>
> My name is John Jobseeker and I am a recent graduate of Success University. We haven't met, but I came across your name and contact information as I researched subject matter experts in the field of sports journalism. I am contacting you to respectfully request a short informational interview with you. As my goal is to one day become a sports journalist, the intent of the interview would be to learn more about the

Introduction: The introduction serves three purposes: (1) introduces you; (2) explains how you obtained the prospective interviewee's contact information; and (3) briefly explains why you have contacted them. The total length of the paragraph should be no more than 4-6 sentences, or about 90-120 words. If someone referred you to the reader, be sure to mention that up front as well. If you are exploring opportunities in another division within your current workplace and you are reaching out to a hiring manager (or whomever), mention that you work in XYZ division and that you are interested in learning about their area of operation. Below is a sample of what the introduction might look like.

> **B**ottom
> **L**ine
> **U**p
> **F**ront

As you can see, the example is clear and fairly concise (about 120 words), and addresses the threeareas identified above. When it comes to the introduction, your goal is to capture the reader's attention quickly so that they keep reading. It is also important to strike the right tone of humility and deference, as demonstrated in sentences 3 and 4 of the paragraph. The introduction serves to give the reader the bottom line up front (BLUF). You never want to make your reader guess what it is you seek of them; be up front. You also do not want them quietly wishing that you would get to the point. Once you have done that, it's time to go into detail on the who, what, and why.

Body: The body is where you will tell the reader about what you are trying to accomplish, why you reached out to them specifically, and what you hope to gain from the interview. Because the body contains the "meat" of the message, it's going to be a little longer than the introduction. I would recommend, however, that you confine the body to one paragraph, no more than 10-12 sentences, depending on their length. This may seem like a short paragraph but that's exactly the point; it's supposed to be. Remember, this is an email, not paper correspondence. Email is meant to be consumed quickly. You do not want annoy the prospective interviewee by forcing them to expend too much effort reading your message.

A good way to open the paragraph is by *briefly* telling the reader about your current situation. However, if you are unemployed do not disclose that, as this automatically sends a message that you are looking for a job. One of the few exceptions is soon-to-be or recently graduated students. Even in this circumstance, you would use a subtle approach. For example, you might say something like:

"Having recently graduated, I'm in the process of exploring career options..." For all other unemployed people, you might frame it along the lines of**"Having most recently worked at XYZ Company, I am interested in exploring the ABC company, or industry".** Obviously, your situation will dictate. There is neither need nor time to go into the details of how you arrived at your current station. All they need to know about is your goal. You can expound on the details of your situation during the informational interview. Once you open the paragraph, you can go into the details of what you are hoping to achieve career wise. Feel free to briefly summarize your background as it relates to your goal, but keep it short.

As you researched prospective interviewees, you may have uncovered information about them that can be useful to you, such as shared interests, unique hobbies, same previous employer or schools, etc. The body is where you would highlight this information, but be brief. Do not focus too heavily on highlighting any commonalities as if that information is your golden ticket. You do not want to appear disingenuous and have your motive viewed as transparent—as though you have an ulterior motive. A subtle acknowledgement of the shared interest is all it takes. Frame the shared interest as a pleasant coincidence and move on.

As you are composing your message, you will want to address how and why you contacted them specifically. Keep in mind that people want to know that you did not just randomly pull their name out of a hat. They want to feel special, and you are much more likely to receive a favorable response if you give the impression that you targeted them specifically for their expertise. As a reminder, appealing to one's ego can be an effective tactic. Your message might sound something like this:

"As I conducted a search of industry experts to interview, your profile stood among the most impressive. I am certain there is a great deal I could learn from you about how to position myself for success. My goal would be to confer with you about the complexities of this dynamic field so that I might apply a more strategic approach in how I pursue my goal of becoming a sports journalist."

From the sample above, you can see that it addresses why I reached out to them specifically and what I hope to achieve. Of course, you can feel free to phrase the message as you see appropriate. One of the most important things to remember, however, is to be straightforward. Even if it is within your capabilities to do so, do not try to dazzle the reader with flowery language and your savant-like grasp of the dictionary as you will only come off as pretentious. Keep it simple and remember to use Plain Language. If you are unfamiliar with the Plain Language concept, I strongly advise you to study up on this and quickly incorporate it into your communication style as you move forward. Trust me; your readers will appreciate it.

Closing: While the introduction and body set the tone of the message, the closing may be the most important. Why? Because the closing leaves the reader with final impressions about you. A good closing can help seal the deal, while a poor one can seal your fate. A well-crafted closing will: (1) reiterate your interest in learning from their expertise; (2) thank the reader for their time, and also acknowledge their busy schedule; (3)

thank the reader for any consideration they may be willing to extend; and (4) inform them that you are willing to accommodate their schedule and preferred mode of interview (e.g. face-to-face, Skype, telephone).

Constructinga well-written, persuasive letter is not difficult. It just requires you to understand and conform to a few principles. While it is impossible to take into account everyone's unique situation in providing sample dialogues, you should be able to gain a sense of the intent of the message from examples above. All you would need to do is simply tailor the message to your situation. Lastly, while there may be a temptation to attach your resume to the email, do not do this—ever. Having someone send you an unsolicited email is one thing. Having someone send you an unsolicited **resume** is another. This is not only bad etiquette but also highly presumptuous and will most likely result in serving no other purpose than grating the recipient. Never ever send an unsolicited resume to someone you do not know well. During the informational interview, you will have an opportunity to ask the interviewee to review your resume, which is actually part of the strategy. However, as is the case with everything else in life, there are ways to do things and ways **not** to do things. Sometimes knowing what **not** to do is just as important as know what **to** do.

Characteristics of a Well-written Letter

In order to aid in developing this type of letter, I have provided list of important principles to consider. Be mindful that it takes practice to construct a good message that inspires people to act on your behalf. There are people whose sole job is to craft these types of messages, and they get paid a lot of money for it. While you may not be an expert writer, following the principles outlined below should help you construct a message that makes a favorable impression with the reader.

Free of errors: This goes without saying, but I'm saying it anyway. Make sure you proofread your work several times. A helpful practice is to read the message aloud. This helps catch inadvertently added words and also helps you analyze the flow of the message (i.e. how well it reads).

§ **Correct standards of writing:** I know this is starting to sound like a broken record, but remember that you are a professional sending professional correspondence to another professional. In this regard, it must conform to correct standards of writing, to include grammar, punctuation, sentence structure, etc. If it does not, you will not be taken seriously.

§ **Maintain a business tone:** Keep in mind that this is business. The reader is not your buddy, Additionally, your message should not resemble an overly sentimental Hallmark card either. You are making a professional request. Your tone should be respectful, friendly, and business-like.

§ **Know your audience:** This is probably the first rule of writing. Write to your audience, taking into account everything that you know about that person, including their position (if known). Also, use industry jargon as appropriate to your audience, but don't overdo it.

§ **Proper titles:** Be sure to address people by the correct honorific, using Mr. or Ms. (Mrs. if known), or professional title, such as Dr. (MD or Ph.D), Chairman, Ambassador, etc.

§ **Do not beg:** There is no need to convey the sentiment that the success of your career hinges on whether they grant you an interview. Your message should convey the sentiment that the prospective interviewee can certainly add **value**, but not that their blessing will make or break you. You are making a simple business request.

§ **Use plain language:** Keep your message simple and easily understood. Do not use complex, strung-together sentences; keep them short and easily digestible. Similarly, there is no need to prove how smart you are by using a bunch of big words. Keep in mind that even smart people appreciate a simple, easily understood message.

§ **Follow up only once:** Once you send the email to a prospective interviewee, follow up no more than once. Persistence is great, but you do not want to e-stalk people. If someone doesn't respond to you after the second attempt, then let it go. I recommend waiting at least two weeks before sending a follow-up email.

§ **Conduct a peer review:** Have someone you trust review the message and offer feedback. Make sure you instruct them to assess message content, clarity, grammar, flow, tone, etc. Remember, there is absolutely nothing wrong with having someone review your work; it's actually the wise thing to do. A second or even third set of eyes can catch what you or someone else may have overlooked.

§ **Take your time:** If it takes you all day to draft the perfect email, it's okay. The last thing you want to do is rush your work simply to get it out the door. Do not waste all the work you have done up to that point by sending out a poorly constructed message. You want to make certain the reader understands that you are someone to be taken seriously. Take great care to ensure your work reflects that assumption.

§ **Appropriate sign-off:** Every letter you send (whether hard copy or email) requires a professional sign off. For example, many people will just use "Sincerely", or "Respectfully", and so on. There are several dozen types of sign offs that account for varying degrees of formality and informality. The important thing to keep in mind is that this is business correspondence. If your sign off is inappropriate relative to the nature of the correspondence, it can raise an eyebrow and have people question your judgment. This may seem like a small thing, but the sign-off offers a glimpse into how you think.

Chapter 18: The #1 Mistakes To Avoid During An Interview

It's great to be prepared for your interview, but if you walk in with a rigid platform of five talking points that you want to address, you risk missing the boat on what the employer is looking for. Sure, the interview is an opportunity to market yourself and make potential employers want you, but you must also be open and receptive to their viewpoint. Really listening to where the interviewer is coming from may reveal exactly what they are looking for.

A job interview is essentially a conversation between two professionals -- a give and take. The best way to be both engaged and engaging is by participating in what we call "active listening".

Never interrupt!

Don't talk while the interviewer is still talking, and if he or she pauses, as if to find the right word, don't jump in with your own words. Wait a few seconds to let the other person gather his thoughts. Your intention may be to help, but it may appear that you're just rushing him or her by filling in the blanks. Be respectful and wait your turn.

Be fully aware of the question.

It's easy to get lost in your own mind-world of how you just asked the last question, or what the diploma on the wall says, or what-have you. But the best way you can honor your interviewer and really get what they are after is to give each question your full attention.

Many times, we listen with the intent to respond instead of to understand. But being so focused on your response can shift your awareness and you could miss some really valuable information from your interviewer. Give your mind permission to wander after you have fully taken in the question.

Restate the question before responding.

Rephrasing the interviewer's question works in two ways: If it's a question you never expected, it can give you some time to think of a proper response. It's also a way to convey to the other person that you are actively trying to understand his or her query. Remember that you don't have to do it every single time, as that could be distracting.

Ask questions.

After doing your research, have a list of questions on hand so that you have something to say once the interviewer is done asking you questions. It shows that you have been listening and are interested in actively taking part in the conversation.

The best way to handle this is to plan and prepare your questions at least a few days in advance. You can practice active listening with a friend, colleague, or relative to hone your listening skills further.

Play the mirror game.

Mimicking your interviewer's movements shows that you are indeed participating in the conversation. Follow his or her tone of voice — the pitch, the speed. But a word of caution: Copy only the good gestures and not the bad (e.g. finger-tapping).

Chapter 19: How Not To Obsess After The Interview

The interview is over and you can't help but fell a release of tension. You made it through and it wasn't as awful as you thought it would (or maybe it was, but hey it was a good experience). Now, you might think you are in the clear and all you have to do is wait. While it is true that waiting is the next step, it is not that easy. Some even find it more difficult between the time the interview has been completed to the time they hear back from the company on whether or not they received the position. Don't continue to go over your interview answers again and again because if you look for flaws you will find them. It is unnecessary torture. Keep yourself busy and if you are on a serious job hunt, continue with your search and put the interview on the back burner until you hear back. If you determine that you provided any wrong information that would be crucial to a decision you may want to consider following up to correct it, depending on what it was. If it was for a driving job and they asked if you have had any speeding tickets in the past three years and you said yes but later discovered it happened four years ago – definitely call. If on the other hand, you were quoting sales results and underestimated the number of sales you made; it would probably be best left as it was.

Keep yourself busy as you wait for an answer from your interview. And if it happens that you didn't get the job use it as a learning experience. If there were questions you wished you would have answered differently at least you know that now for the next interview you attend.

How To Express Thanks To An Interviewer

You may think that it's advantageous to follow-up with an interviewer to thank them for their time and keep your name in the forefront of their mind. While this may have that affect on them, it may not be in the positive way you are thinking. An interviewer takes time out of their regular job to fill vacancies in a department. It is an extremely busy and stressful time for them and they do not want (nor have time to) take calls from everyone that they have completed interviews with. Sending a think you is not altogether a bad idea but it depends on the method. If you received a business card, send a quick e-mail to thank them for their time and that you are looking forward to hearing from them. Make it quick and to the point and leave it at that. Do not expect a reply because you probably won't get one and do not follow-up on your e-mail to make sure they received it – you will become an annoyance.

Second to sending a quick e-mail, you can send a short and professional thank you note. The message should be similar, thanking the interviewer for taking the time to sit down with you, express how much you enjoyed speaking with them and learning more about the company. It may not guarantee you the job, but thank you notes, if done the right way, may open doors for you in the future. If there are openings in the company at a later time, the interviewer may remember you and think of you before others.

Chapter 20: After The Interview

At the end of the interview, always verify a time and date that you can expect to hear from the organization and whether to expect a call, text, email or other form of communication.

Thank You

Go home and write an a short but thoughtful thank you email or letter. Take a few minutes to express your gratitude for the opportunity. If there was something that you especially enjoyed or left a lasting impression on you, let the interviewer know.

Writing a thank you note keeps you fresh in the interviewer's mind as he or she considers hires. It also demonstrates more of your soft skills from the ability to follow-up, to interpersonal and communication skills.

Contact

If you don't hear back by the appropriate time, contact the organization. Maybe they lost your contact information or sent an email to the wrong address. Either way you have the right to know and they have an obligation to be accountable.

Getting the Job

If you get the job, congratulations. Confetti for you. Life is good. You can stop reading!

If on the other hand, you're offered the job, but it just doesn't feel right, don't take it. If you come to this conclusion before you hear back from the potential employer, reach out to them and let them know, you've decided to go another way. Potential employers appreciate honesty. By letting them know, you may be saving them time and energy. In the end, you are the one that must live with the decision. If you take a job that you know you're going to miserable at, and quit or be fired in a few months, you're wasting everyone's time. It's not fair to employers who don't want to train someone only to have them leave. And it's not fair to you, who will be stuck doing something you hate instead of chasing that dream job you really want.

Something Better Out There

But what if you get door number three? What if you don't get the job? Know that it's not the end of the world. If you have the opportunity ask what made them go with another candidate, or what you could have done differently. There's never shame in asking questions for self-improvement.

You may want to take a few minutes or perhaps the evening to collect yourself. When you're ready, reflect on the interview experience and what you learned from it. Consider what you could have done better and improve for next time.

If in your heart of hearts you feel there truly is nothing you could have done better, don't waste sleep over it. Always remember interviewers and employers are people too. Sometimes it comes down to personality or the kind of day they had before they made their decision. As Howard Schultz, former CEO of Starbucks says, "Hiring people is an art, not a science."

Elon Musk uses a very personal criteria in making his hiring decisions. "If you have a choice between a lower valuation with someone you really like, or higher valuation with someone you have a question mark about, take the lower valuation."

Just remember, life is all about how you choose to look at things. Look at the choice not to hire you as an opportunity to find something even better. Your perfect job is still out there somewhere, just waiting for you to find it.

Chapter 21: Preparing For Your Job Interview

Job interviews consistently rank as one of life's most stressful events, right up there with divorce, death of a loved one, and major surgery. But I am going to share with you two important points that will quell the heart-pounding, stomach-churning feeling that often goes on during an interview. They are ...
• Be prepared; and
• be prepared

Once you do both of these things, it will make interviews much easier, so much so that you may even look forward to them.

When I say to get prepared, it means a couple things, but most importantly, do research on the company you are interviewing with and even research the person interviewing you. There is so much information available online nowadays. Know what value you can add to the company. Also, don't worry about being nervous. If I see an interviewee is nervous,

I try to put them at ease. There is nothing wrong with being nervous. If the interviewer asks if you are nervous, be honest. The fact that you are nervous shows that you care about getting the job.

Be on time for the interview. Punctuality is important and shows respect. It is disrespectful to be late for anyone ever. If someone is late for an interview, there is a good chance they will not be hired. But likewise do not be an hour early! Just be on time or 5 to 10 minutes early.

Get some sleep the night before. You do not want to arrive looking like you have celebrated someone's stag do of hen's night the night before.

- Prepare for interview questions
- Prepare to talk about yourself and your accomplishments in your work and non-work life
- Prepare with information about the employer you are interviewing with
- Prepare to ask questions of your own

You've already made one excellent step forward in reading this book, so congratulations—you are on your way!

Think of the interviewer as a "fearful" person. Perhaps the interviewer fears that ...

• You won't be able to do the job.

• You are able to do the job, but just won't come in often enough.

• You are able to do the job, but just aren't willing to devote much time or thinking to it.

• You are able to do the job, but will quit so soon it'll make his head spin.

• You have some terrible flaw that he was supposed to ferret out during the interview.

• You will cost the company a lawsuit or put it on the six o'clock news.

• You may drive the company nuts.

It helps to think of the interviewer in this light, because it puts you inside his head and gives you a sense of what he is looking for, trying to avoid, and, what's worse, trying to do under pressure.

It is very good practice to try being the interviewer—seeing things from her perspective. It can be interesting to see how interviewees think on their feet and answer questions, and many times, to see what not to do. Give it a try with your friends.

Mistakes

The number-one mistake hiring managers say job-hunters make is a lack of research about the employer, the job, and sometimes even the industry. It simply drives interviewers nuts when an interviewee knows little or nothing about the company or organization and the products it makes, services it sells, or causes it champions, and the top competitors and challenges it faces in today's market. Yet it's frightfully common, and a job-hunter armed with knowledge about the employer, job, and industry has an immediate edge over much of the competition.

Research is the key word in job interviews, just like location is in real estate. Research the employer, industry, and job to the hilt, so you'll be prepared to answer questions and ask good ones.

But that's not the only mistake. Here are the top five mistakes job-hunters make in interviews, according to a survey by CareerBuilder.com.

1. What They Say (or Don't Say)

The biggest mistake is how job-hunters communicate, whether it's discussing their personal problems instead of answering or asking questions about the employer, sounding as if they're robots reading a script, answering in monosyllables, or bad-mouthing ex-bosses. Some blurt out real bloopers, like the job-seeker who wanted the position because it offered health insurance, or the customer service applicant who confessed to not being a "people person."

2. How They Act

The second biggest mistake is how many job-seekers act, from downright rudeness like answering cell phone calls during the interview, arriving late, biting fingernails, and even starting to munch on a sandwich.

3. Bad Attitudes

Job-hunters who display no enthusiasm—about their current or previous jobs, or the one at hand—don't score points, nor do those who keep looking at their watches during the interview, or those with egos of heroic proportions who don't admit to ever making a mistake.

Enthusiasm is a trait highly valued by interviewers. It often trumps more experience and even better skills, since employers tend to feel skills and experience can always be developed over time, but a good attitude and eagerness to do the job can't be taught.

4. How They Look

Bad grooming and dress is another mistake interviewers frown upon, whether it's facial piercings, poor hygiene, visible tattoos, hair in peculiar colors, or casual dress like jeans and T-shirts. The young generation likes tattoos, but many business owners like me do not. That is not to say that I don't have great staff with tattoo's, I do. But just hold back on getting one on your arm or leg. If you have do get a tattoo, let it not be too visible.

5. They're Dishonest

Lying about their current or past jobs, degrees, knowledge, or criminal record and exaggerating their achievements are ways some job-hunters are dishonest. Not to mention the applicant who stole an object from the interviewer's office.

Chapter 22: Interview Skills Introduction

In today's business world, the ability to successfully interview for a new employment position is the overall primary element that will typically lead to an offer for employment. Though resumes, education, skills, years of experience, and advancement records, play an important part in the employment process, the fine line between obtaining a new job, or losing out on it, truly comes down to your interviewing skills. With career moves, and the necessity to change jobs from time to time, as well as widespread company restructurings that force individuals to seek new employment, the development and maintenance of your interviewing skills is something that will serve you well should you find yourself in need of new employment.

With so many people out of work these days, and an economy that still struggles to rebound, the number of employment opportunities, in comparison to the number of individuals who are actively seeking employment, are truly tipping the scales. Employment opportunities are abundant in some fields, while they are very limited in others, which is an indication that candidates need be aware of the competition out there, and put a great deal of focus on their ability to perfect their interviewing skills and ace their interview. Your personal presentation during an employment interview is very much a firsthand representation of your character, ethics, poise, professionalism, ambitions, motivation, strengths, and weaknesses, each of which are closely viewed, and rated by your interviewer.

Whether your first time interview is with a recruiter, or with the human resource personnel within the company you are applying to, it is every bit as important to make a good, lasting impression, from start to finish, as you journey through the interview process. Take appropriate time to brush up on your interviewing skillset before you head out for that all-important first phase interview, and give great attention and practice to the following useful interviewing tips.

1. Always arrive early for your interview. It is advised, by the experts, that people should make a point to arrive fifteen minutes in advance of their scheduled interview time. This sends the message that you are remarkably organized, and recognize the value of your interviewer's time. When greeting your interviewer be certain to offer a firm handshake. Never use a slight or timid touch.

2. Throughout your interview be certain to act both professionally, and naturally. Having direct eye contact with your interviewer, emphasizes your interest, and showcases your confidence. When speaking, it is very important to use a strong speaking voice and not be too passive. Again, this will emphasize your confidence, and also affords your interviewer the respect earned as they conduct your employment interview over the extended period of time.

3. Always be sure to answer questions with a positive approach and response. This indicates to your interviewer that you are focused on resolutions and not problems. Employers are always in search of candidates that are capable of handling situations, and making things better. Troubleshooters and problem solvers are the candidates that every interviewer and new employer is in search of to add to their professional team.

In summation, it is important to recognize the value and the impact your "perfect interview" can have on obtaining the job you are actively pursuing. Confidence, poise, direct eye contact, a strong speaking voice, a firm handshake, positive responses, and a noticeable familiarity with the parent company's history, are all important factors that come into play when interviewing. If you add a slight bit of charm to your conversation, and pleasant facial expressions throughout your interview, then indeed you will capture the interest and attention of your interviewer in an incredibly positive light.

Each of these critical elements when delivered with a professional, yet natural presentation will assuredly make your interview, and personal presentation stand out far above the rest.

The candidate that is recognized in the first phase interviewing process is typically the candidate that is apt to find himself or herself on the receiving end of an attractive job offer when the entire interview process is concluded. To come out the victor in the rigorous challenge of interviewing is, without a doubt, only the first of many accomplishments that will be achieved as you move forward on your journey to employment and career success.

Chapter 23: Possible Answers Just To Guide For Interviewees.

All moving machinery if any, fans, air conditioners to be shut down immediately. Inform fire brigade, police, your chairman or Chief person of the company. Operate fire extinguishers, water sprinkler systems and any other devices to control fire, Opening up of all doors and windows, Moving all staff and employees from the building. All emergency exits to be kept open. These are the fundamental action that should be immediately taken. If possible all valuable assets to be removed immediately

First of all we have to speak with the employees concern and find out what's the cause for their sudden decision. If it's a matter that can be settled under your purview, you should make every effort to satisfy the workers, at least to get the decision postponed, until it's reported to higher authorities.

Inform HR department and allow them to do a preliminary investigation. Taking the ledgers, cash registers and other important documents and equipment in to company custody with the help of HR manager. Taking statements from the persons involved. When required suspending the work of people said to be involved, until further inquiry.

The questions that an interviewee can ask from interview board

At the final stage of interviews interview board gives an opportunity to the interviewee to ask any questions from them. This is a very professional practice. When you are not given any chance to ask anything from them, you must take the initiative and ask whatever you have to ask. It's aright of an interviewee. You should never be reluctant to raise any questions to them, but it should be in a very decent manner. Before accepting or signing any agreement with employer, you should perfectly know all about the job position, terms and conditions etc. Just to help people who sit for interviews, we will discuss about some important questions that should be asked in an interview.

How many hours I have to work for a week as per conditions? Do you pay over Time for extra hours perform?

What's your method of Performance Evaluation Management? Should I know something about criteria etc?

If I accept the job, would you in future insist me that I should work in a distance branch within the company?

I wish to know about my salary package & other benefits in detail. When I reach the top of my present salary point by gaining annual increments, would you upgrade me?

Have you planned for any company expansions, opening up of new establishments, branches or any other business developments for next year? If so may I have a general opinion?

Can you just point out the worst/ difficult areas to function in this job position? What are your major problems company and this department facing right now at present?

Do you have a policy of promoting staff within the company for suitable positions? If so what made you to advertise this position?

On accepting the job may I know whether any avenues are there to rise up in my carrier path? I mean can I groom myself within the company for better prospects.

Letter of Appointment / Terms & Conditions

On acceptance of the job position you will be served with the letter of appointment, in which all terms & conditions applicable to your employment will be in black and white. It is advisable to read and understand the contents of the letter before you sign the employment contract. Very seldom even there can be some sort of discrepancies in the letter. Some times terms will differ to what you have agreed upon in the interview or the salary mentioned in the letter may not be what you expected. So, it's of immense important you read several times and understand the contents before you sign employment contract.

Shall we now discuss about contents of an appointment letter in brief. It is interesting to study about pre interview and post interview procedures because if you intend passing an interview you must compulsorily have comprehensive knowledge about interviews. Each and every employer is legally bound to serve with a letter of appointment to all employees. Following contents should be clearly expressed in an appointment letter or in a contract job appointment.

The name of employee, designation and nature of the appointment

The grade to which the person is appointed

Basic remuneration and the scale of remuneration Whether remuneration is paid weekly, fortnightly or monthly Cost of living allowance or any other allowances, if any.

The period of probation or trial, if any, and the conditions governing such period of probation or trial Conditions governing employment and termination Normal hours of employment. Number of weekly, annual, casual, maternity holidays and privilege leave if any over time rate payable Provision of Medical aid, if any.

Conditions governing any provident, pension schemes or gratuity scheme applicable to the employment Prospects of annual bonus and promotions

Industrial safety & accident policy

Industrial safety is a condition covered under government Industrial Act of any country.

Organizations, factories come under industrial sector, should be well covered under this law.

Following are some guide lines for you to establish in your memory. Whenever you are facing Interviews in industrial sector, this information will help you to pass the interview.

Every moving part of prime movers, transmission machinery and every dangerous part of other machinery should be guarded.

Practical steps should be taken to prevent any person falling in to vessels, structures, sumps or pits which contain dangerous liquids either by covering or fencing them.

Employees engaged in hazardous, work should be provided with suitable protective equipment such as gloves, goggles, ear protectors, respirations etc, as necessary.

Female workers should not be employed in cleaning or lubricating any machinery which is in motion.

Hoists, lifts, cranes and other lifting machines should be protected and also be tested periodically by a competent person. Safe loading weights should be indicated in such machines.

Suitable steps should be taken to prevent fires, and explosives in processes which could give rise to accumulation of dust, gases or vapor.

All doors in a factory except the sliding doors should be constructed to open outwards - such doors should not be locked or fastened in such a manner that they cannot be easily and immediately opened from in side.

Accident Policy

The company owners and occupiers of factories should have their own laid down accident policies to be covered under the country's employment law. They should have an insurance policy with accident compensation benefits, to cover all employees working in an industrial organization. Authorities of the organizations have to give written notice of any industrial accident which results in the death of a person or disables a person from earning his full wages for a period of over 3 days or makes a person unconscious as a result of heat exhaustion, electrical shock or inhalation of un-respiration or poisonous fumes or gasses. An insurance policy to cover such risks to be obtained from a recognized insurance organization and they should be informed in writing promptly in such accident. Also all records of accidents to be maintained in the premises.

Chapter 24: Interviewing The Interviewer

During every interview there comes a time where you are allowed to ask a question, provide additional information or lead the conversation down a specific path of your choosing. You should never let these opportunities pass you by. You should always be thinking at least one or two steps ahead. So as this interview winds its way down you need to make your final appeal for further consideration and learn a few things that might help you further down the road.

Here are a few things to consider when asking questions of the interviewer and getting additional information out in the open that might have otherwise gone unnoticed.

Interview Handouts & Other Information

We discuss this in more detail in "Resume Hacks" but sometimes there is just not enough room in a resume for all the education, experience and accomplishments you might have to offer.

So to make sure all or any of that extra information is not lost in the shuffle, you can create "fact sheets" that include any relevant information and bring them along with you and present them to the interviewer.

I like to wait until we are discussing my accomplishments and experience and then I present them with the fact sheet saying to the interviewer "Her are some more of my accomplishments and background that you might find helpful." The result is the interviewer not only can look at the information now but it will likely be included in the information folder about me when it moves up the line to someone else.

Just make sure that whatever you give the interview has distinct relevant information pertaining to the job you are interviewing for. Do not bore them with unrelated details or how which scoring records you set while in High School. Only relevant information should be included.

Salary & Benefit Issues

Money usually does not come up in the first interviews unless the subject is raised by the interviewer. Do not bring it up yourself as this is not the place or time. The only exception might be if the next step in the process involves considerable travel or commitment and you would not want to invest that in a job that paid far less than you expected. But even then, you can raise that topic when you know you are going to the next step.

Benefits are another issue as they are usually gone over quickly during the interview as a way of giving you a bit of information pertaining to the company. They are not gone into in-depth but are presented at an overview level.

As you go further into the process meaning a second or third interview, then benefits and salary become part of the process and are negotiated between the company and the applicant. If the job is being decided on the first interview discussions might be held then or be done over the telephone as the offer is made.

Your Questions for the Interviewer

You will usually be asked if you have any questions and you can use this opportunity to address any points you thought might not have gone as well as you hoped or if you had thought of anything new as the interview progressed. Questions can help in the transition between topics you wish to expand on.

For example, you might ask if the interviewer had any specific concerns about your background or abilities. This can be useful in two ways. If you are moving ahead in the process you can take the time to address those concerns and possibly turn a concern into a strength. If you are not moving forward you would know of potential weaknesses that you might wish changing or addressing in the future.

If something about you that is important or impressive was somehow overlooked or not acknowledged by the interviewer ask a question designed to direct the conversation in the direction. Such as "I noticed in the job posting you mentioned experience in managing remote employees. Did you notice that in my current job I manage a remote field staff of 28 people and have done so for 10 years? During that time we hit almost every goal and exceeded all expectations." This gets the information out there and can help establish you as the premier applicant or candidate.

You should use this portion of the interview to show a passion for the position and the company. Share a few ideas or ask probing questions that highlight your interest in the job. Show your excitement so the interviewer gets the feeling that this is more than a paycheck for you. Don't go overboard but make sure the interviewer sees your excitement and passion.

Ending the Interview

Eventually all good things must come to an end. When all the questions have been asked and the interviewer is confident that they have all the information they need at that point in time, they will signal the end of the interview.

Regardless of how the interview had gone and whether you feel you did a good job or a poor one, than the interviewer with a smile and remain positive. Keep in mind that it is not your opinion that matters now but the opinion of the interviewer that counts. Don't make any excuses or apologize for doing poorly even if you feel that way. Such statements can only reflect negatively upon you and possible raise doubt in the mind of the interviewer.

If it feels right you can inquire as to what the next step in the process might be and when those decisions are likely to be made. If the interviewer wishes to let you in on that information he or she will do so. If not, they will just tell you that someone will be in touch with you. Don't push then about this. Just accept the answer they give you and move on.

Thank the interviewer for taking the time out of their day to talk to you and tell them you enjoyed the experience even if it was comparable to hell on earth. You want to appear calm and confident as you end the interview just as you did when you walked in. Keep your head up, keep eye contact and thank the interviewer again.

Then leave the office, thank the secretary or receptionist or whoever else is there and leave the building. Keep up the confident exterior and smile all the way until you're out of the building. Sometimes there are cameras you know and who knows who might be watching.

If a sound a bit paranoid please excuse me but I always believed that the little things make all the difference in the words and if something is possible, act like it is and you will rarely be disappointed!

Now you can relax and drive home or out to lunch or wherever you're going and start the next part of the process. Oh, I'm sorry. Did you think you were done now that the interview is over? Well some people might be done.

But you're not. Not by a long shot.

Chapter 25: Leave Your Questions For Last

"One important key to success is self-confidence. An important key to self-confidence is preparation."——Arthur Ashe

"Do you have any questions for us?' "Ehm...No". Sound familiar? This is the mistake most job hopefuls make when the interview is about to end. Interviewers ask that question for a reason! NEVER LEAVE THE ROOM WITHOUT ASKING QUESTIONS. It's their way of figuring out whether you actually thought out and did some research about the position and organization before applying for it. It's also a way of finding out if you have initiative and are proactive in your thinking.

Yes, you are allowed to ask questions of your own, both during and after the interview. This will also help you lead the interview in the way you want it to go (as mentioned before) which can prove to be a good thing if it had not been going so well earlier in the interview. Don't get me wrong though, that doesn't mean that you can ask just anything that pops into your mind!

Ask your questions in a casual manner to avoid looking desperate and NEVER argue with the interviewer. It's been proven that interviewers appreciate the quality of questions YOU ask more than the answers you provide. The following question types are some you should think about asking your interviewer:

Questions About The Company

Now, they will assume that you've done your research regarding their company's profile before you came to the interview. Your sources will probably include online forums, an official website (if they have one), business directories etc. You may have even chatted with their employees to get a more personal outlook on the company. In short, this is information you should have been able to research quickly without wasting their time asking about it.

What should you ask then? It's really simple. Those questions should be about

information that's not covered in the material you were able to gather like:
Why is the position open?
Why did the previous person leave?
What are your plans regarding cutbacks and what effects will they have on the department?
How important is this position to the general operations of the organization?
How many people have left the position in the last 5 years?
Why is there a high turnover of employees for this position?
What do I have to do to get promoted?
How many employees got promoted from the position in the last 5 years?
What are the most important qualities required to effectively man this position?
What are their expectations?
What's the company's opinion on work environment?
Will I receive any formal training?
Of course, these are not the only questions you may ask, but they're a good point to start. Asking well thought out questions can swing the entire interview

your way even if it wasn't going so well earlier on. It shows intelligence and initiative, believe me, no employer is ever averse to those qualities. Remember, employers are usually on the lookout for those individuals who actually know what they're talking about. They also like those who show a can-do attitude regarding the position being offered.

Why should you ask questions? Asking the above mentioned questions will show them that you're serious about the position and will work hard to make the company meet its objectives. Not only will they appreciate your efforts, but they might even think of promoting you faster than you think (IF you deliver on your promises of course).

Questions About The Position

As a rule of thumb, it's safer to avoid questions about the company. The best bet is to stick to questions about the role being interviewed for. Now you have to come to the job itself. These questions have to be focused mainly on the day to day activities that the job requires and what you might expect to encounter. Start off with any of these:

Can you tell me more about the type of clients/data/equipment I'll be working with?

What's my supervisor like? (How he/she handles projects).

Does the position require frequent changes/improvements? If so, then how?

Will there be any major challenges to worry about? How can I handle them?

Will I be expected to travel? If so, how often will I be expected to do so?

What can I do to improve my chances of being promoted?

When can I expect to hear from you?

I already have some ideas in mind? Would you like to hear them?

Can I see examples of projects I might be handling if you go ahead to hire me?

From your perspective, how do you see this position contributing to the overall success of the company?

How do you see me as a candidate in comparison to the ideal candidate for this role?

Can you give me this Job? (Only ask this question if you're feeling especially confident of your performance. It could very well backfire and seem as cocky but it could also come off as being bold, an attribute some interviewers will appreciate.)

Is there any aspect of my resume or qualifications we have discussed in this interview that might give you any reservations about my ability to handle this job? (This question can be crucial if you sense there are still some doubts in the mind of your interviewer. It gives you the chance to work on your interviewer's mind and turn things in your favor. The interviewer will usually bring up any such areas of doubt and you'll have the chance to play it down while highlighting other areas where you have an advantage.

Most interviewers will answer yes to the final question, but ask it ONLY if you have a good plan of action already mapped out! This is where it pays to really do your research before the interview. A good way to do this is to keep in mind all the buzzwords he/she used when describing the company. Add your 2 cents worth by suggesting ideas that can help them increase sales/ productivity or improve punctuality for instance anything that will increase results and profits. Make sure to keep your strengths and weaknesses in mind when giving this sales pitch though. You'll be expected to meet the high standards you've set on your ideas if you're hired.

Questions about Work Environment

Getting that dream job won't do you much good if you hate the people you end up working with. Once you land that position, the people you work with, the way your work is evaluated and the way the management supports or trains its employees will have a huge effect on your performance. Not only will your dream job not look so heavenly, but your anxiety and tension levels can shoot through the roof if all these issues aren't quite right. Nip the problem in the bud by asking the following questions:

Can you tell me anything about my co-workers?

Can you tell me anything about the management and the people who work in it? What's their performance been like?

Should I be on the lookout for any office politics? If yes, then what exactly would you say I could look out for?

Are there any special plans or arrangements for employees who are also students? How are they managed?

What's your performance evaluation system like?

Will the company support me if I decide to get some training from outside?

Is there a support system for employees who want to further their education?

Why do you like working here?

I cannot stress this enough but DON'T MAKE PROMISES YOU CAN'T KEEP and don't let the adrenaline rush cloud your judgment. You may impress them enough to hire you, but what happens when you fail to live up to those high expectations? Being fired is a much worse than not being hired. Make your life easier by remaining as close to the truth as possible. You'll make a better impression that way.

Salary and Benefits

Normally most people will tell you to avoid asking questions about salaries and benefits you might receive until after the interview. They're right. Asking about medical insurance for instance before they hire you may make you out as a greedy person.

On the other hand some employers may bring up the issue themselves. Your job will be to ask questions IF they do so, but try not to be too eager if you know what I mean. Telling them right off the bat that you have a large family to support or a truck load of bills and student loans to pay off won't help you get any sympathy votes either.

It will be a whole different ball game if you're being offered the job though. This is the time when you should bring up your expected salary. Word to the wise, try and talk in terms of range rather than a single salary figure if you can help it. This will allow both parties some room to maneuver and negotiate a sum that would be mutually acceptable. Try researching the sum others had in that position and how you are qualified to get more for instance. There are many online resources you could use to get an idea of the average salaries for that position. Payscale.com and salary.com are useful in helping you have an idea of what salaries to expect for that job position.

Remember what was said about asking about the performance evaluation? That will come in pretty handy when salary raises are being considered. Keeping an eye on that point system will also help you hone your own skills according to the job, which can only spell good news for your future prospects

You have to take a bit of a different stance for benefits though. Try not to ask about any during or after the interview. However, if you just can't control your curiosity, then ask in a way that doesn't make you out to be desperate. You're better off knowing whether they offer them or not as compared to what they offer for instance. Very few companies don't have a benefit plan for their employees anyway.

Chapter 26: The "Unemployment" Job Description

In this economy, it is seemingly difficult to find *any* job, let alone a career. Surprisingly, though, the job market has an abundance of open positions awaiting applicants. If unemployed, your job is to apply to as many open positions as possible. Make it a point to work full-time searching through job openings and submitting your application. This is your opportunity to start a new path in life; view this opportunity as a chance to start over and try any profession you've ever wondered about working.

Join a Job Posting Website

There are many job websites out there available free of charge. Some of my favorites are www.monster.com or www.careerbuilder.com, though there is an unlimited number. Most sites have the same postings, so signing up for one or two is sufficient. There are also job sites devoted to specific industries.

www.malakye.com focuses on job postings within the action sports industry, making it easier for employers and job seekers with the same interests and talents to be united. If you have a specific company in mind that you'd like to apply for, you should go directly to their website to see the available openings and application process.

Take the time to set up a strong profile for yourself and be open to different job categories that you haven't yet explored. You should look at any job openings that sound interesting to you; even if you don't have all the skills or experience the employers are looking for in an applicant. The more doors you prop open, the more opportunities you create for yourself.

Set a Daily Application Goal

Every day, get your cup of coffee, a hearty breakfast, get dressed and head off to your office (even if that's just your couch). Don't let yourself lounge in your pajamas or sweatpants, as your attire will reflect your attitude. Set yourself up to be confident, aggressive and successful in your search for a job.

Set a daily goal for getting out applications. Remember, your full-time job is searching for openings and applying for positions, so set the goal high to fill your workday. Again, apply for any and all positions that intrigue you or capture your attention. Commit your allotted "work" time to searching and applying for jobs, but after the work day is done, take a rest.

Continue or pick up some hobbies that will take your mind away from the application process, if only for a few hours. Attend your cardio or yoga classes regularly, go on a bike ride, walk your dog, or even pick up a skill like knitting. All these extra activities will continue to challenge your mind, help you to maintain a healthy lifestyle and clear your head to start fresh the next day.

Now take into consideration the specific set of skills that you have. Many postings will have specifications or requirements for the applicant, such as a certain certificate or degree needed. These requirements are set for the applicants because they are non-negotiable for the job being offered. Focus on your own areas of talent and apply to positions that you believe you can confidently offer to employers and you will find that your preference of positions will begin to narrow. This is not to say that you shouldn't branch out to explore other openings, but to apply for a physician position without a medical degree is just a waste of time.

After a while, it becomes exciting to get on the websites and see what new positions have opened. Routinely applying for new job openings not only puts yourself out to potential employers, but also helps you to learn what your strengths are and how you can personally contribute to different positions.

Sometimes it helps to create a work atmosphere for yourself rather than sitting at home. Drive to your local coffeehouse and set up your workspace at one of their tables. This forces you to have an acceptable appearance, a more focused mindset, and a determination to get your work done (all while having the added bonus of a delicious mocha latte).

Use All Resources

While applying for positions online is quick and successful, make sure you are exercising all of your resources for finding open positions. Look in the local newspaper, network with family and friends, and visit local job fairs. You can always walk into a business that you are interested in working for and inquire about any open positions. It is *okay* to be more aggressive when looking for a job. This economy makes for an extremely competitive environment and your initiative to be a strong voice for yourself will only better your chances at landing that interview or job.

Two of my past positions were found by reaching out to my family and friends to let them know I was looking for a job. In one case, my sister received an email from a manager of a company she had interned for in college. He was looking to fill an entry-level position and was asking for referrals from his database, which contained all of his clients, friends and employees, past and present. I had no prior experience in the industry, but was eager to learn.

The brief introduction from my sister, followed by sending in a well-written cover letter and resume highlighting my skills that paralleled the position description landed me the interview. My enthusiasm and determination landed me the job. Coincidentally, while I was at the same company another position opened and the manager again, reached out to his database for referrals. Make sure your friends and family know you're looking — those connections can lead to golden job opportunities.

Lastly, don't be afraid to start in an entry-level position. An entry-level position is a great way to start with a company and demonstrate your set of skills. Learn the business by asking questions and taking on all responsibilities that are offered. As you establish your value at the company, you will easily start to climb the ladder of promotion.

Conclusion

I really want to thank you for reading this book. It's my hope it has helped you prepare well for your upcoming job interviews. It's also my hope that, more than just preparing well for them, you'll be able to ace those interviews and land your dream job.

Half the battle is knowing the questions and answers shared in this book. The other half is preparation. I highly encourage you to prepare by asking a trusted family member or friend to conduct mock interviews using the questions you've read here. It's one thing to know the answers to these questions; it's another to know how to communicate those answers in ways that show humble confidence and capability. With practice and preparation, you have what it takes to WIN your dream job!

www.ingramcontent.com/pod-product-compliance
Lightning Source LLC
Chambersburg PA
CBHW072003070526
44583CB00015B/1315